THE WARSAW GHETTO'S
LITTLE NURSE

THE WARSAW GHETTO'S
LITTLE NURSE

THE MEMOIRS OF ALINA MARGOLIS-EDELMAN

EDITED BY IRENA GRUDZIŃSKA-GROSS

INTRODUCTION BY MARCI SHORE

TRANSLATED BY LUDMILA MELCHIOR-YAHIL

CENTRAL EUROPEAN UNIVERSITY PRESS

CEU PRESS

© English translation by Ludmila Melchior-Yahil, 2026

Published in 2026 by
CENTRAL EUROPEAN UNIVERSITY PRESS

an imprint of Amsterdam University Press

E-mail: *ceupress@press.ceu.edu*
Website: *www.ceupress.com*

ISBN 978-963-386-864-5 (paperback)
ISBN 978-963-386-865-2 (ebook)

A Cataloging-in-Publication (CIP) record is available
from the Library of Congress.

Contents

Editor's Preface

Irena Grudzińska-Gross

I always knew that Alina Margolis-Edelman (1922–2008) was stoic and determined. I had an early connection with her: I heard from my mother that, as a toddler, I was a patient of Alina's mother. My own mother was then studying medicine at Łódź University with Alina and her husband Marek Edelman. A hero of the armed anti-Nazi insurrection at the Warsaw ghetto, Marek is much better known than his wife; since she emigrated with their children to France in 1971 while he remained in Poland, they spent a great part of their lives apart. Like Marek, she was a doctor and devoted her life to helping the sick. She went out of her way to work in war zones and alleviate the lot of poor and abused children. And although she was a no-nonsense person, I would define her deeds with an old-fashioned expression: concern with the suffering of innocents.

Alina's life story is truly dramatic. The very dates of her birth, youth, and adulthood encompass war, occupation, and persecutions. Born into a polonized Jewish family of doctors, she begins her memoir by presenting her childhood in the vibrant city of pre-war Łódź. It is an image in sepia—that of a world which will be destroyed as of September 1939. Already in the second short chapter of the book, we seem to witness a scene of childhood molestation. The adult Alina will choose the medical specialization of pediatrics and work on, among other things, the detection and prevention of the abuse of children. She was a daring pioneer.

It is hard to find among Jewish stories of survival a description of the Warsaw ghetto school of nursing. The running of that school and the way it was kept going through the worst times of the ghetto's existence is an outstanding example of the everyday courage, stoicism, and resistance not only of the adults but also of the teenage girls learning the trade. In her recounting of it, Alina maintains the innocence and naivety of her teenage experience and makes this episode of her life an exemplary and moving one. This is only one of the moments that the reader will find memorable in her book.

Her memoir, unfortunately, does not talk about her postwar times, and I especially regret not hearing about her co-founding and working for the French humanitarian organization Médecins du Monde. The bulk of her memoir is about the Second World War, and her take on it is very original. Her voice is simple yet very absorbing, and her storytelling is seemingly quick but of great profundity. The reading of this short memoir will take almost no time, but the reader will be very affected. We meet here a great person speaking with modesty of her truly heroic life. The things that happened to her, her decisions, and her actions are presented without an ounce of boasting or pretension. Quite the opposite; she consistently undervalues herself. She met with great hardships and difficulties, and she faced them with courage. And she succeeded in bringing help to those who needed it most. A life to learn from.

Though I was born after the war, its violence and cruelty overshadowed my life and the life of my generation. Our parents either did not say anything about it or talked about it all the time. I wish Alina's book were written when I was young, but then she was saving the world rather than writing. For me, however, her memoir continues her mission, and I have always thought it should be read as widely as possible. There have been many other persons who have shared this idea: her children, her translators, and her supporters – both from Warsaw and Łódź and from the United States and France. This is what moved me and Marci Shore to propose this memoir to the present publishing house. The book is out; now it is the reader's turn.

Introduction

Marci Shore

"Ala has a dog named Ace" [1]

Alina Margolis-Edelman was one of the great women of the 20th century—behind the scenes, as it were. She lived through multiple worlds, radically different from one another, some barely remembered today. The setting for her childhood was the factory city of Łódź, the site of the robber baron capitalist drama captured in Andrzej Wajda's 1975 film *The Promised Land*. Wajda based the film closely on Władysław Reymont's 1897 novel of the same name, and it was Wajda, a friend, who persuaded Alina to write this book. [2] The Łódź of *The Promised Land* was a Polish, Jewish, and German city in the Russian tsarist empire. [3] Alina's parents were woven into this linguistic tapestry of Polish and

---

1   For conversations about Alina Margolis-Edelman and insights into her life, I am grateful to Irena Grudzińska-Gross, who shepherded this English translation through publication, as well as Anna Bikont, Konstanty Gebert, Irena Grosfeld, Izabela Kalinowska, Aleksander Smolar, and Alina and Marek Edelman's children, Aleksander and Anna Edelman.

2   Andrzej Wajda, "Ala ma kota," September 2, 1995; https://wajda.pl/film/ala-ma-kota/. "Jestem nigdzie," Natasza Kozłowska-Coudert, interview with Alina Margolis-Edelman, *Tygiel Kultury* no. 3 (1998): 18–24; https://edukacjafilmowa.pl/ala-z-elementarza-2010/.

3   See Yedida Kanfer, "'Each for His Own': Economic Nationalism in Łódź, 1864-1914," *Polin: Jews in the Kingdom of Poland, 1815-1918*, ed. Glenn Dynner, Antony Polonsky, and Marcin Wodziński (Liverpool: Liverpool University Press, 2014), 153–80.

Russian and Yiddish and German. Her father studied in Heidelberg and Strasbourg, her mother in Bonn and Petersburg-turned-Petrograd, where the Bolshevik Revolution found her in October 1917. Alina, born in 1922, was only four years younger than the Second Polish Republic itself.[4]

Alina's parents were assimilated Polish Jews and, above all, physicians. Her mother was a pediatrician who loved to socialize and had little time for her own children. Among her many friends was the Polish pedagogue Marian Falski, who authored the reading primer *Elementarz*. Falski wrote Alina— "Ala"—into his book, and *"Ala ma Asa"*— *Ala has a dog named Ace*—became an iconic phrase, the first sentence generations of Poles learned to read and write. The book's cult-like status has now lasted a century and renders the original title of Alina's memoirs—*Ala z Elementarza* ("Ala from the Reading Primer")—untranslatable.[5]

Alina's father, Aleksander Margolis, was a Bundist. To say this was to say something that at one time meant very much. In 1897, the same year the First Zionist Congress was held in Basel, Switzerland, the Jewish workers' movement named the Bund formally convened in Vilna. A center of Jewish culture, Vilna was then predominantly a Polish, Yiddish, and Russian-speaking city in the tsarist empire; during Alina's childhood it was known as Wilno, a city in Poland, and today it is Vilnius, the capital of Lithuania.[6] The Bund was a secularist, Yiddishist, socialist party. After the Bolsheviks consolidated power to the east, the Bund concentrated its activities in Poland, allying not in-

---

4   Justyna Dąbrowska, "Nie ma rzeczy niemożliwych," *Tygodnik Powszechny*, June 14, 2011, https://www.tygodnikpowszechny.pl/nie-ma-rzeczy-niemozliwych-139551.

5   Roman Pawłowski, "Ala ma Asa. Kim był człowiek, który nauczył miliony Polaków czytać i pisać," *Gazeta Wyborcza*, September 1, 2021, https://wyborcza.pl/ 7,175991,27517412,ala-ma-asa-kim-byl-czlowiek-ktory-nauczyl-miliony-polakow. html; Mikołaj Gliński, "Marian Falski, autor kultowego 'Elementarza,' urodził się 130 lat temu," *culture.pl*, December 7, 2011, https://culture.pl/pl/artykul/marian-falski-autor-kultowego-elementarza-urodzil-sie-130-lat-temu.

6   See Cecile Kuznitz, *YIVO and the Making of Modern Jewish Culture* (Cambridge: Cambridge University Press, 2014) and Mordechai Zalkin, "Vilnius," trans. Barry Walfish, *YIVO Encyclopedia of Jews in Eastern Europe* (2010), https://yivoencyclopedia. org/article.aspx/Vilnius.

frequently with the Polish Socialist Party and calling for cultural autonomy for Jews within a Polish state. In the debate with the Zionists between *doykayt* ("hereness") and *dortkayt* ("thereness"), the Bund stood firmly on the side of *doykayt*: the future of the Jews was *here*, in Poland, alongside their non-Jewish neighbors.[7]

Today, the teleological deceptions of retrospect make it seem a foregone conclusion that the Zionists would win the contest with the Bund. Yet this was in no way the case during Alina Margolis's childhood. On the contrary, in the 1920s and 1930s, the Bund had a program that arguably sounded much more sensible, grounded, realistic: a Jewish workers' party allied with a larger labor movement, a Jewish culture in a language already spoken by most Jews, a future in a place where Jews already lived, alongside people they already knew. From the perspective of the time, much more fantastically unrealistic was the Zionist idea that millions of East European Jews would adopt a new vernacular language, uproot themselves *en masse*, and resettle in an unfamiliar climate, in a Middle Eastern desert amongst cacti and camels, amidst people about whom they knew very little.

Today the Bund is largely forgotten. It was the road not taken, the world that might have been—had history not happened otherwise. Alina was seventeen when Nazi Germany invaded Poland. Suddenly her father's old friend from his student days in Heidelberg appeared at the door of her home in Łódź. Hans Werner was now an officer in the Wehrmacht—and Alina's Germanophile father was delighted to see him again. History was not indulgent towards this rekindled student friendship: in November, Alina's father was taken by the Gestapo. Alina would bring food packages to the prison camp; one day the guard allowed her to see her father. And Aleksander Margolis wanted

---

7   See Antony Polonsky et al., eds., *Polin: Studies in Polish Jewry*, vol. 9, *Jews, Poles, Socialists: The Failure of an Ideal* (Oxford and Portland: Littman Library of Jewish Civilization, 2008). The *YIVO Encyclopedia* is also a very good source on the Bund and related topics: Daniel Blatman, "Bund," trans. David Fachler, *The YIVO Encyclopedia of Jews in Eastern Europe* (2010), https://yivoencyclopedia.org/article.aspx/Bund (accessed 2 June 2024).

to know from his daughter: were they doing something for him? Could they not somehow secure his release?

"Mama has been trying, and Mr. Werner has been trying, but there's nothing to be done."

Shortly afterwards, Aleksander Margolis was executed as part of the Nazi decapitation of the Polish intelligentsia. And for the rest of Alina's life, this "there's nothing to be done" remained with her.[8]

* * *

Afterwards, Alina's mother, Anna, left for Warsaw with Alina and Alina's younger brother, Jan (called Olek in the Reading Primer). Alina was accepted into the Jewish Nursing School, which in the Warsaw Ghetto became a microcosm of another, more orderly world: there was discipline, purpose, and solidarity. The pink nurses' uniforms offered some protection from the transports, and in this sense the school was an asylum—if only in a very provisional way. Once, despite her uniform, Alina was caught on the street and taken to Umschlagplatz, where Jews were collected for deportation, and where she waited, paralyzed in the crowd to be herded onto cattle cars bound for Treblinka. Then a young doctor, Adina Blady-Szwajger— "Inka"— saw Alina from a window. She moved to break the window and call out to her; and Alina's mother yelled to Inka not to do it, the broken glass would injure someone, but Inka went ahead anyway—and this shook Alina from her stupor. She ran away, in her pink uniform, up the stairs, to Inka, and to the patients. She saved herself. Later she reflected on her mother's yelling to Inka not to break the glass when this had been the only way to save her—a reflexive response from another time? How could one judge?[9]

---

8   Karolina Tatarzyńska, "Ala z Elementarza dziś miałaby sto lat. Niezwykłe życie Aliny Margolis-Edelman," *Gazeta Wyborcza*, April 19, 2022. https://lodz.wyborcza. pl/lodz/7,35136,22654124,niezwykle-zycie-aliny-margolis-edelman-ala-nie-tylko-z-elementarza.html.

9   Alina Margolis-Edelman, interview with Anka Grupińska, "Myśmy tam żyły jak w jakimś azylu," *Tygodnik Powszechny*, April 2004, https://www.tygodnikpowszechny.pl/mysmy-tam-zyly-jak-w-jakims-azylu-125305.

It was one of many moments difficult to judge. On April 19, 1943, when most of the Jews from the ghetto had already been gassed in Treblinka, a group of Jewish resistance fighters—young activists, Bundists, communists, and Zionists—rose up to fight the Germans.[10] "It was only a choice as to a manner of dying," Marek Edelman, a Bundist and one of the uprising's commanders, would later repeat.[11] He was among a handful of the insurrectionaries who survived, escaping through dark sewers where they nearly died of thirst, waiting for days for Polish communist partisans to take them to hiding places. Marek was among those who went on to fight in the second uprising, the Warsaw Uprising, in August 1944. These Jewish survivors of the Ghetto Uprising joined Polish communist partisans fighting the Germans—not because they were communists, but because the non-communist Polish partisans were often hostile to Jews. In October, the Warsaw Uprising was defeated; the Germans deported the remaining population of what had been the Polish capital. Marek was among those trapped in the northern district of Żoliborz, hiding as the Germans combed through the mined streets. When a Polish doctor at a Red Cross hospital organized a rescue mission, Alina's mother wanted to go, but was rejected for being too old. And so she sent her daughter, understanding that Alina would likely not return.

Alina did return, carrying Marek Edelman on a gurney, his face covered so that he would not be recognized as a Jew. It was its own peculiar romantic beginning. Soon afterwards, they married. Warsaw, the city of two uprisings, had been burned to the ground, and Alina and Marek moved to Łódź to study medicine. Marek had fallen into a depression then, and treating illnesses proved satisfying in its concreteness. After their time in the ghetto, after the two uprisings, how could any stakes lesser than life and death have any meaning at all?

---

10   On Marek Edelman and the contested history of the Warsaw Ghetto Uprising: Marci Shore, "The Jewish Hero History Forgot," *The New York Times*, April 19, 2013, A31.

11   Hanna Krall and Marek Edelman, *To Outwit God*, trans. Joanna Stasinska and Lawrence Weschler (Evanston: Northwestern University Press, 1992).

For the Jews who fought the Germans in the ghetto, the point was a more dignified death. Marek had never counted on surviving. But someone else had counted on that. Marek's Bundist comrade Zygmunt—whose real name was Zelman Frydrych—turned to him on April 19, 1943 when the fighting began.

"I won't survive, but you will," Zygmunt said.

He had a child, a then-six-year-old daughter hidden at a convent in Zamość, in southeastern Poland. He asked Marek to find her after the war.[12]

In May 1945, Nazi Germany surrendered; the war was over. Several months later, Marek suddenly told Alina that Zygmunt's child had to be found. She had no idea what he was talking about then. But in fact that sentence—*"Trzeba znaleźć dziecko Zygmunta"*—a subjectless phrase uttered several months after the German defeat, would be among the most consequential words they ever spoke to each other.

Elżunia Frydrych was not easy to find. She had been taken to a convent not in Zamość, but in Przemyśl, eighty miles farther south. Adina Blady-Szwajger, the same Inka who had broken the window to shake Alina from her stupor, had later taken Elżunia from the convent and brought her to an apartment in Warsaw, where Elżunia hid until the uprising began in August 1944. Then the man in whose apartment Elżunia was hiding went off to fight, and the man's wife threw the not-yet-eight-year-old girl out onto the street. Along with other homeless children, she was collected by an organization and taken to a town outside of Warsaw; there she was picked up by a miller to look after his geese. Later the miller and his wife, who had not been especially kind, passed her on to a locksmith, and it was at this home that Alina and Marek found her after the war. The locksmith and his wife did not want to give her up. Alina and Marek tried to persuade them, and in the end there was a transaction: Marek and Alina, likely with the help of the American-based Joint Distribution Committee,

---

12   The story of Zelman Frydrych's daughter is told most fully in Anna Bikont, *Nigdy nie byłaś Żydówką. Sześć opowieści o dziewczynkach w ukryciu* (Wołowiec: Wydawnictwo Czarne, 2023).

paid the locksmith and his wife for their care of Zygmunt's daughter and took Elżunia home with them. By the spring of 1946, Elżunia was living with Marek and Alina in Łódź. Soon Elżunia began to call Alina "mama," although Alina, just fourteen years older, was too young to have been her mother.

The war was over, but it was not a peaceful time in Poland. A brutalized population had been made to witness the murder of their neighbors. Many Poles risked—and often gave—their lives to save others, including Jews; other Poles had been implicated in the Nazis' slaughter of the Jews. Sometimes both things were true of the same people. Soviet domination—and Stalinist terror—were encroaching. Many Poles identified Jews with the communists; some had collaborated in the murder of the Jews; many, even if they had not collaborated in the Jews' murder, had profited from it, appropriating Jewish property; and many were not happy to see Jewish survivors attempt to return to their homes. There was chaos, terror, and uncertainty about what would come next as Polish anti-communist partisans fought Polish communists in a developing civil war. And there was antisemitism.

Estera Iwińska, sister of the Bundist leader Wiktor Alter, had been among the Bundists who had looked after the teenage Marek Edelman after the premature death of his mother in the 1930s. Now she came to him with the news that she had arranged for a Bundist family in the United States to adopt Elżunia. Marek and Alina did not want to give her up—the threesome had become a family—but Estera Iwińska was a trusted authority, and she insisted: if Elżunia were to be killed in a pogrom, it would be on their conscience. Moreover, they were students with no money and little means to support a child.

On July 4, 1946, a false accusation that a Jew had kidnapped a Christian child served as a provocation for a pogrom in Kielce, less than 100 miles from Łódź. Forty-two people were killed.[13] By the end of that month, Elżunia was in Sweden, waiting for an American visa and sending letters to Alina and Marek telling them how much she missed them

---

13   See Jan T. Gross, *Fear: Antisemitism in Poland after Auschwitz* (New York: Random House, 2006).

and wanted to return to Poland. She asked them to send a Polish-English dictionary and Polish candy. The candy in Sweden did not compare.

A year-and-a-half later Elżunia joined her adoptive parents in the American suburbs of Westchester, New York. The couple was already over fifty, with grown children, the father adoring, the mother somewhat cool. In any case, Elżunia, after a childhood hiding in poverty and darkness, was now provided with the most comfortable bourgeois conditions for her adolescence. Material comfort, though, had its limitations. In 1948, not yet twelve, she wrote to Alina and Marek from the United States:

> I can say with a pure heart that I'm now living normally and lacking for nothing, and yet from time to time I become horribly sad, like I want to bite and scratch everyone around me, and I feel as if I were lacking something after all, although I don't know what. Most often, it happens in the evening and doesn't end until the next morning. I try to calm myself down, of course, but that's usually very difficult.[14]

In 1951, five years after Elżunia's sudden appearance and disappearance in their lives, Alina and Marek's first child, Aleksander, was born. In 1956, Alina gave birth to his younger sister, Anna. By then Marek had become a cardiologist, and Alina a pediatrician. They were concerned above all with life-and-death situations, not with the everyday of childrearing. Once, when the children were still small, just barely starting school, Alina received a medical fellowship in France. She left them for nearly a year, trusting that food, shelter, and good health would be sufficient in a mother's absence.

On the other side of the Atlantic, Aleksander and Anna's might-have-been older sister came of age as a beautiful and charming young woman who spoke accentless English and graduated at the very top of her class. Elżunia learned French and Latin, wrote poetry, completed her undergraduate degree at Cornell University, and went on to do a master's degree in literature at Columbia University. There she

---

14   Quoted in Bikont, *Nigdy nie byłaś Żydówką*, 48–49.

met Robert Dallek, a graduate student in the history department. They married in 1959. Three years later, while on vacation with Robert in Mexico, Elżunia checked into a hotel room and took an overdose of sleeping pills. It was 1962 and she was twenty-five years old.

* * *

Aleksander and Anna were not without some muted jealousy towards the girl who might have been their adopted older sister. Elżunia was their parents' first child, to whose loss—twice over—their parents never reconciled themselves.

Six years after Elżunia's suicide, the Polish communist regime blamed student protests against censorship on Jews disloyal to Poland. Many of the students were "of Jewish origin," the children of the Stalinist elite, and many were imprisoned. Upon their release, they were pressured, insofar as they did not want to return to prison, to leave the country. The "anti-Zionist" campaign of March 1968 eventually saw the emigration of some 13,000 Polish citizens, mostly Polish Jews from the intelligentsia who very much identified as Poles. Those who remained often lost their jobs. Alina was not permitted to submit her habilitation thesis; she was made to understand that she would not be able to pursue her medical research on childhood diabetes, an illness with a high mortality rate at the time. Her children were harassed and threatened at school. And so she left for France, taking Aleksander and Anna with her, while Marek remained in Łódź. Emigration to the West was more than difficult; it was degrading. Polish medical degrees were not accepted in France; now a refugee in her mid-forties, Alina was forced to requalify as a physician. She wanted to return to Poland—but Marek insisted she and the children remain abroad; no one knew what would come next in Poland, especially for Jews. Her children felt how deeply the humiliation in France penetrated her.

But she did not accept defeat. She passed all the French medical examinations, requalified, established herself, and as soon as she got her bearings, turned to helping others. Both Alina and Marek—still formally married, now on different sides of the Iron Curtain—became godparents of sorts, advising, mentoring, and supporting the milieu of students from the generation of 1968 who had led the protests.

One of those students was Barbara Toruńczyk; she had been imprisoned in 1968, and after her release, became an activist in the Polish opposition and an editor of underground publications. When General Wojciech Jaruzelski declared martial law in Poland in December 1981, Toruńczyk went to Paris. In the beginning, she felt terribly intimidated by France. Yet she went on to become a legendary editor of the émigré literary journal *Zeszyty Literackie*. This was only possible because Alina, drawing upon her French citizenship, registered *Zeszyty Literackie* in her own name, taking all the nontrivial financial and legal risks upon herself.[15]

This was not Alina's most dramatic or most generous act. During martial law in Poland, she organized assistance for the opposition. She was among the original activists of Doctors without Borders and later Doctors of the World. She traveled the globe, volunteering for missions in El Salvador, Chad, Afghanistan, and elsewhere to treat victims of civil wars and starvation. In Africa, mothers brought her their emaciated babies. In the South China Sea, she rescued Vietnamese fleeing communist Vietnam and provided medical care to children on boats. She was capable of thinking quickly, finding ways around the rules, and improvising solutions. In Bosnia, she organized help for rape victims; in Saint Petersburg, she arranged care for homeless children.[16]

When she would return to Paris between missions, she and Barbara Toruńczyk would visit museums and jog through Parisian parks.

Alina had found professional success in France. Her Jewishness remained a given to her, as did her Polishness. She felt a particular affinity for El Salvador, and when asked whether she considered herself Polish or French or Jewish, she often felt tempted to say "Salvadoran."[17] She never severed ties with Poland—on the contrary, she co-founded SOS,

---

15 Barbara Toruńczyk, *Żywe cienie* (Warsaw: Fundacja Zeszytów Literackich, 2012).
16 On homeless children in Russia, see the remarkable 2005 Polish documentary film *The Children of Leningradsky* (*Dzieci z Leningradzkiego*) by Andrzej Celiński and Hanna Polak.
17 *Ala z Elementarza*, director Edyta Wroblewska, Poland 2010.

a French-Polish organization to support Polish doctors and Polish medicine. After the fall of the Iron Curtain, Alina created a foundation in
Poland to support children who were victims of domestic violence and
sexual molestation—at a time when sexual abuse was not a subject of
public discourse. Herself long silent about her own experiences, she
now wrote a medical textbook about battered child syndrome.[18]

The fall of the Iron Curtain saw not only the opening of communist party archives, but also a broader breaking of silences. Barbara
Toruńczyk became a midwife to Alina's memoirs and, as an editor,
a discoverer of Alina's unsuspected literary talent. The discovery of
unsuspected literary talent applies as well to Alina's Czech contempo-
raries, Heda Margolius-Kovály and Miloslava Holubová, two of the
other great women of the twentieth century, survivors of Nazism and
Stalinism, moving unobtrusively amidst history in all its savagery,
only sparingly and belatedly telling their stories.[19]

*   *   *

When Marek visited the United States in the 1960s, not long after
Elżunia's suicide, Elżunia's adoptive father implored Marek to tell him
why she had done it. They had given her everything. Marek did not
know what to say.

No one then spoke of post-traumatic stress disorder, of intergenera-
tional trauma and guilt. No one could have lived unscathed through
what Elżunia did as a child: the separation from her parents, who did
not survive the war; the cruelties of the convent, where the children
were beaten by the nuns and where she was made to care for still
younger girls, toddlers whom she could not protect; the multiple
changes of families and identities and rules; and the terror and the

---

18   Alina Margolis-Edelman, *Zespół dziecka maltretowanego: diagnostyka medyczna* (War-
      saw: Fundacja Dzieci Niczyje, 1998).
19   See Heda Margolius-Kovály, *Under a Cruel Star*, trans. Helen Epstein (New York: Holmes
      and Meier, 1997) and Miloslava Holubová, *Necestou cestou* (Prague: Torst, 1998).

hiding—no amount of subsequent privilege could vanish that trauma. But there was, perhaps, no language to speak about that then.

Alina and Marek never spoke with their children – Aleksander and Anna – about the war. They never spoke about Treblinka, about Auschwitz, or about the two uprisings in Warsaw in which they had both taken part. Aleksander learned about the Warsaw Ghetto Uprising only when he was an adolescent and found a copy of his father's early account, *Getto Walczy* (The Ghetto Fights), in the library. Anna was younger. It was neither of her parents, but rather her nanny who read that book with her.

As Irena Grudzińska-Gross, another student activist who reluctantly left Poland following her imprisonment, points out, Alina's literary style is elliptical: many things are alluded to but never articulated to the end; the vignettes are filled with blank spaces. As in a Chekhov story, there is no moral, no instructions from the author as to what conclusions the reader should draw. The meaning of what is not-fully-said necessarily changes with temporal distance—"understanding with half-words," as the Russian expression holds, was not necessarily something that could be passed on to future generations. The present world, moreover, is one less of silences than of talking in excess.

It has never been easy to convey understanding about experiences so far beyond the realm of the everyday. Marek spoke to Hanna Krall about the Ghetto Uprising only thirty years later.[20] Yitzhak Zuckerman, Marek's Zionist comrade from the ghetto resistance, told his story around the same time—on the condition that the tapes be transcribed and published only after his death.[21] Michał Głowiński wrote of his childhood in the Warsaw Ghetto only in the 1990s, after the death of his parents, so as not to make them revisit those times.[22]

---

20 Hanna Krall, *Shielding the Flame: An Intimate Conversation with Dr. Mark Edelman, the Last Surviving Leader of the Warsaw Uprising* (New York: Henry Holt, 1977).

21 Yitzhak Zuckerman, *A Surplus of Memory: Chronicle of the Warsaw Ghetto Uprising*, trans. and ed. Barbara Harshav (Berkeley and Los Angeles: University of California Press, 1993).

22 Michał Głowiński, *The Black Seasons*, trans. Marci Shore (Evanston: Northwestern University Press, 2005).

Kristine Keese, related to Barbara Toruńczyk through her stepfather and Michał Głowiński's contemporary in the Warsaw Ghetto, wrote only in the twenty-first century, when she was nearly eighty.[23]

"God is trying to blow out the candle," Marek told Hanna Krall, "and I'm quickly trying to shield the flame, taking advantage of His brief inattention. To keep the flame flickering, even if only for a little while longer than He would wish. It is important: He is not terribly just. It can also be very satisfying, because whenever something does work out, it means you have, after all, fooled Him..."[24]

God was there, Edelman teasingly suggested, *but not on their side.*

Alina's style of self-expression was less sarcastic; all the same, like Marek, she did not believe in God. And she regretted, perhaps more than he, that her parents had not raised her to be a believer—believing in God would have made it easier to live, after all, and easier to die. How else could one cope with this mutilated world?[25] For Alina, engaging was coping: to act was both transitive and intransitive—it was to shape the world and to shape oneself; to help others was to help oneself.[26] Humans, horribly imperfect, as both she and Marek knew, had nothing else to rely upon apart from one another. It was by means of the work she did to save others that she saved herself, she told the filmmaker Edyta Wróblewska.[27]

Irena Grosfeld, also among the milieu of godchildren and the post-1968 emigration to Paris, saw Alina for the last time several days before her death. In the hospital now as a patient, Alina spoke to her about Elżunia.

"She never made peace with it," Irena Grosfeld said.

---

23   Kristine Rosenthal Keese, *Shadows of Survival: A Child's Memoir of the Warsaw Ghetto* (Boston: Academic Studies Press, 2016).

24   Krall, *Shielding the Flame*, 85.

25   See Adam Zagajewski, "Try to Praise the Mutilated World," trans. Clare Cavanagh, *The New Yorker*, September 17, 2001, https://www.newyorker.com/magazine/2001/09/24/try-to-praise-the-mutilated-world.

26   See Cardinal Karol Wojtyła, *The Acting Person*, trans. Andrzej Potocki (Dordrecht: D. Reidel Publishing Company, 1974).

27   See the film *Ala z Elementarza*, director Edyta Wróblewska, Poland 2010.

Before the War

The Reading Primer

Mr. Marian Falski[1] was a great friend of my mother's.

He was a tall, handsome gentleman with slightly wavy, graying hair and a friendly smile.

On my seventh birthday, he brought me a beautifully wrapped gift. It was the *Reading Primer*.[2]

On the top left corner of the first page he wrote: "For Ala—from the *Primer* author," and a bit lower:

"Ala ma kota"—"Ala has a cat."

---

1   Marian Falski (1881–1974), Polish educator and educational activist. Falski was a member and activist of the Polish Socialist Party (PPS) prior to the reestablishment of Poland in 1918. In the Polish state he worked for the Ministry of Religious Denominations and Public Enlightenment. After 1945, he headed the Office of Research and Statistics of the Ministry of Education of Poland until 1950. In 1954, he became a member of the Polish Academy of Sciences.

2   Falski published his popular *Elementarz powiastkowy dla dzieci* (Reading primer for children) in 1921. It replaced an earlier primer he had written in 1910 called *Nauka czytania i pisania* (The science of reading and writing). Subsequent versions of the *Elementarz* were published for urban and rural children, for soldiers, and for illiterate civilians. It was republished in 1945 as *Elementarz dla szkoly wiejskiej* (Primer for village schools) and went through various transformations afterward. It is longest-published pedagogical work of its kind.

Miss Julia

When we lived in the old apartment on Piotrkowska Street[3] and my brother wasn't born yet, I was cared for by Miss Julia. The two of us lived in the part of the apartment nearest the kitchen. I call it "lived" because this was where we spent most of our time, almost never stepping into the front part.

The apartment was on Łódź's main street, on the third floor of an old turn-of-the-century building and had two entrances: one at the front and the other from the kitchen. The front stairs were decent and wide, though not as luxurious as in some other town houses. The kitchen stairs were narrow, worn out, and neglected. From the front, you entered the hall and then went on to two large, pretty rooms. The kitchen stairs led straight to the kitchen. A long, narrow, dark corridor connected both parts of the apartment. Next to the kitchen were a bathroom and a pantry, and across from each other, two small bedrooms. Miss Julia occupied one of the small bedrooms and I, the other. This way she could easily hear if I woke up at night.

Every morning, we went for a walk. At the main entrance, we always passed the janitor of our building, the mustachioed Mr. Franciszek. Mr. Franciszek had a very fat wife and a lot of children, who—I didn't know why—did not want to play with me.

Every evening, Miss Julia put a footstool in the middle of the kitchen and a big bowl on top of it. She filled the bowl with warm water. This was my bath. I had to sit quietly so as not to splash the floor when Miss Julia meticulously washed me with a pink or blue washcloth. I couldn't understand why she never washed me in the bathroom tub. Anyway, when all naked, I would stand up in the bowl so Miss Julia could wash my tush. There would be a knock on the door, and then Mr. Franciszek would be standing there. Even though this took place every evening, each time I felt myself blushing in shame. I was, after all, totally naked and defenseless. Then Miss Julia would wrap me in a white towel, put a long nightgown on me, and carry me

---

3   It is the main thoroughfare in Łódź and one of the longest in Europe.

to the bed in my room. She would leave the door ajar, so I wouldn't get scared.

Through this half-open door, I would watch Mr. Franciszek sneak into Miss Julia's room. He was red-faced and panting. Miss Julia, in his arms, was squeaking like a mouse.

Then I would fall asleep.

My Parents

From the very beginning, everything seemed to indicate that the life anticipated for my mother[4] would be strewn with roses. She was beautiful, radiant, smart, intelligent, talented, and her father's beloved daughter.

Grandfather was a respected merchant, quite successful. He lived in Warsaw and, like many merchants of his time, did business in Poland and Russia, mainly in St. Petersburg. In a portrait painted in those days, he looks more like a Polish nobleman than a Jewish merchant, with a wide mustache turned up at the ends. Free evenings he spent at home, playing a card game called *Preferans*[5] with his best friend, a priest.

All the children, and he had five of them, received higher education: two daughters became physicians, one a violinist, and another studied chemistry, while the only son graduated from engineering school in France.

Mother was the apple of grandfather's eye. When she was ready for the last grade of her Warsaw high school, he sent her with grandmother to St. Petersburg, where—as it was believed—the level of education was particularly high. There she got her high school diploma and was preparing for medical studies.

---

4   Anna Margolis née Markson (1892–1987).
5   Preferans, or Préférence, is a 10-card plain trick game usually played by three players with a 32-card deck. Originating from Austria, it was once one of the most popular card games in Central and Eastern Europe.

When on October 25, 1917,[6] she heard shots, she ran—like everybody else—to Nevski Prospect to see what was really happening in the city. The streets, as she told us later, were drowning not in blood but in the red wine that people were taking from the luxury shops.

Hiding her diploma in a shoe, she managed to get to Warsaw.

Grandfather immediately sent her to study in Bonn, known for a flourishing student life. She had only one problem: Professors in Bonn did not accept female students, so mama and her friend from Paris, who were the only two girls there, had to listen to lectures sitting on the floor behind rows of desks—hidden by the backs of their classmates. Whenever a professor noticed a female student, he would stop a lecture and leave the classroom.

Every Sunday they traveled to Paris to learn the tango, which was just becoming fashionable.

She came back to Poland with a doctor's diploma. Grandfather, however, did not live to see it. She started working at the Anna Maria Children's Hospital[7] in Łódź, which today is named after Janusz Korczak.[8]

Almost immediately, two brothers, both young doctors, fell in love with her. She chose my father.[9] She fell into the frenetic world of work. She became a pediatrician, an expert on childhood tuberculosis. She worked at the hospital, in schools, at the clinic for poor children, and even received patients at home.

Mama was a social activist kind of doctor, and she acted as such in all circumstances that life threw at her. At the same time, she was

---

6   October 25, 1917: The start of the Bolshevik revolution in Petrograd.

7   Established in 1905, the Anna Maria Children's Hospital was one of the most modern children's hospitals in both Poland and Europe at the time. Its construction and operation was financed by wealthy citizens of Łódź and it remained open during the Second World War.

8   Janusz Korczak (1878—1942), Polish-Jewish pediatrician, pedagogue, and children's author. A children's rights advocate, Korczak drafted a children's constitution in 1919. In 1911, he became the director of Warsaw's Dom Sierot, an orphanage for Jewish children. He remained in charge of the orphanage until 1942, when he was deported to Treblinka and perished along with his orphans.

9   Aleksander Margolis (1888-1939).

full of the joy of life; she could party until the morning, dancing, playing the piano, and entertaining guests.

No wonder that she rarely saw us. Sometimes my brother, looking from the window, would ask:

"Do you think mama will come to us today?"

Father also did not take care of us at all, yet he seemed tender in
his own way. Supposedly, when I was a baby, he carried me in his arms
at night to stop my crying. He called my brother, Olek, by the nick-
name "Olutka," and when he was home, he shared his daybed with us,
and even though he would fall asleep in an instant, it was nice. He
also had a say in important matters. For example, during the academic
strike organized by the Jewish youth in response to the persecution
of Jewish students, he did not let me go to school, even though I was
only in second grade.

My father was a handsome man — tall, with dark hair and clear,
blue eyes. He was a physician and the director of a big hospital in
Radogoszcz,[10] a part of Łódź. He received patients at home, and
though he did not speak a word of Yiddish, he was also an activist in
a Jewish socialist party, the Bund.[11] He wrote all of his speeches and
articles in Polish and then had them translated. Because of this work,
he served a term on the socialist town council in Łódź as councilor
responsible for public health in the last years before the war.

All this took a lot of his time. Still, he read a lot, and every second or third day he sent me to the library to exchange borrowed
books. On his free evenings, he played the piano, with the music
sheets always above the keys. Sometimes he played four hands with
mama. He liked opera, especially Wagner. He listened to it on the
radio, always looking at the score. He was a true representative of the

---

10   Originally a village located on the outskirts of Łódź, Radogaszcz became a part
      of Łódź following German occupation, with its name changed to Radegast. The
      Germans established a transit camp in the district in July, 1940.
11   The General Jewish Labor Bund in Poland (*Ogólno-Żydowski Związek Robotniczy
      "Bund" w Polsce*) was a secular Jewish socialist party established in December 1917.
      The party promoted the political, cultural and social autonomy of Jewish work-
      ers, and fought against both anti-Semitism and Zionism. It was dissolved in 1948.

prewar intelligentsia—broadly educated, with interests beyond his professional field.

He did his medical studies in Heidelberg. When in a good mood, he would sing student songs, such as *Alle Rosen duften, Alle Rosen duften, Nur Mat-rosen duften nicht!*[12] and others like it. This brought back a picture of a town brimming with academic youth, humor, and songs.

From time to time, father was visited by other important activists. He would tell me that these were very wise men and that I should remember them well because not every child was so lucky as to see them up close.

Miss Julia served them dinner in the big front room, and when they finished, they were not to be disturbed under any circumstances.

It happened sometimes, however, that in the middle of the night, father would come to my bedroom and carry me in his arms, still asleep, to the salon filled with heavy cigarette smoke. When I awoke, he would say, for example, "So, tell the gentlemen what the capital of China is?" I would say "Peking," the gentlemen would laugh, and father, proud as a peacock, would carry me back to bed.

My parents had many friends. They often went out in the evening or entertained at home. I would get out of bed and peek through a keyhole at what was going on. Sometimes they danced, and I noticed that my father usually danced with the same lady. She was a good-looking, small, blond woman with a nice, pretty smile.

One night, I couldn't fall asleep. A ribbon on my nightgown got undone, and my mama wasn't there to tie it back. Suddenly, I heard a loud conversation and mama crying. On my toes, I walked to my post at the keyhole. Mama was very agitated. Father was explaining something and telling her she was right. I was shivering from the cold. It lasted a long time; then I got back to bed, and while falling asleep, I understood.

---

12   "All roses smell, all roses smell, only sailors don't smell..." A variation of a song from the theatre comedy *Die Näherin* by Ludwig Held from 1880, with music by the Viennese composer Carl Millöcker.

At that time, I had a friend, Irka Pchła. Pchła, which means flea in Polish, was not her real name, but she was so tiny and frail that it really fit her. We were inseparable. I told her my sorrows. She understood them very well—she had experience. Her parents did not live together. Her father had some other lady who didn't even try to play the part of a mother.

We decided to take matters into our own hands before it was too late.

Every morning, we followed my father. After some time, we'd learned his entire schedule and where he went during the day. From spying on him, we knew that he occasionally had some free time in the early afternoons. It was not hard to discover that, in some distant coffee shop, he was meeting with his blond.

The most difficult part was behind us. What next?

The next day was September 1, 1939.[13]

A few weeks later, father was arrested. The Germans put him, with other hostages, in a camp in Radogoszcz,[14] almost across the street from the hospital where he worked as director.

I went with Irka to the address where, as we'd learned, the blond woman lived. Bursting into tears, I said, "Mama asked me to tell you that tata was arrested by the Germans."

Mama never found out what we had done.

Grandmother, My First Encounter with Death

I had a working mother. Not only working, but also enjoying her life. As a result, I saw her, I must admit, seldom. I was taken care of by Nanny Izia and grandma. Actually, I had two grandmothers: one in

---

13   The start of the German invasion of Poland.
14   A temporary Nazi police prison was established in a local factory in Radogoszcz shortly after the German occupation of Łódź. Its initial inmates were Jews and members of the Polish intelligentsia. It was replaced by a more permanent structure in July 1940 called *Erweitertes Polizeigefängnis, Radegast* (Extended police prison, Radegast).

Łódź and one in Warsaw. I visited the Warsaw grandma on various holidays—until on one occasion, All Saints Day, I came with my friend, Kazik. The moment I sat at the table, I spilled my cocoa on the clean white tablecloth. Grandma changed the tablecloth, spread out a new one, equally white, and told me to sit politely and be careful. The moment I sat down again—real bad luck - I overturned my new cup of cocoa with my right hand and Kazik's cup with my left elbow. After that, I stopped visiting grandma, who clearly did not have patience with children.

So, I was left with only my Łódź grandma. She was short and fat, with a puffy face. She was also diabetic. I don't think she spent much time with me, because I barely remember her. She used to go for treatments to a spa in Druskienniki.[15] Now women are going there for treatments again.

There was a solarium in Druskienniki. On the grass, at the poolside, and on the two terraces, which you climbed up to on some creaky wooden steps, there were old, naked, and obese women—lying, sitting, and soaking in the water. I don't recall any others. They had thick necks and sagging bellies with skin that, when they stood up, fell with abandon, almost to mid-thigh. Others had enormous fat bellies supporting huge bosoms. When they lay down on the wooden floor, their white breasts spread out on both sides, giving the impression they were just lying there slack beside them, unattached.

I teamed up with another little girl, who was also brought there by her grandma, and we chased each other among those bodies, paying close attention not to step with our little sandals on someone's flattened breasts.

The women in the solarium gathered in groups of five, six, or seven, and in these groups—in the water or on beach chairs breaking under their weight—they talked and talked without end.

I hated those trips to Druskienniki, but mama insisted that there was good air there and lots of woods.

---

15 Now called Druskininkai, in Lithuania, located on the banks of the Nemeunas river. A spa resort since the 19th century.

It's funny, but many years later, in a totally different country, on the shore of the Dead Sea, I saw the same women, sitting in groups of five or six or seven on the steps of pools, soaking in the water and constantly telling each other something. They seemed almost to have been transported alive from the solarium in Druskienniki. It was hard to realize that those other women had already been gone for a very long time.

My Łódź grandma also took me with her to the countryside when my parents went on vacation. We always went to some places close to town, like Kolumna near Łódź or Tworzyjanki between Łódź and Koluszki, and sometimes to the so-called "line" near Warsaw,[16] where the air was particularly healthy. Grandma always said, "Alinka, breathe. Mama pays a lot of money so you can have fresh air."

One summer, in the middle of the day, a taxi stopped in front of the wooden summer house where we lived. My father and Uncle Ignaś got out of the taxi. They walked quickly past me, telling me to go play at the neighbors. I felt like crying, but they did not pay any attention to me.

Later, they called me and told me to get dressed. We were going back to Łódź.

Grandma was already in the taxi, with tata on one side and Uncle Ignaś on the other. They left a seat for me near the driver, which was surprising, because they always said that children were not allowed to sit up front.

A few days later, when we were returning from the funeral, there was only one thing in my head: the image of grandma sitting stiff in the cab and not speaking a word to me. I thought and thought and for a long time could not think it through. Until, finally, I understood.

We were walking through a long cemetery alley, and I heard my aunt, whom I couldn't stand, tell someone,

"Look at this child. She hasn't even shed a single tear."

---

16   This is likely a reference to the Otwock line—an area in the south-eastern region of right-bank Warsaw, along railway line No. 7.

My Encounter with Religion

My parents were atheists. They got married in a civil ceremony in Katowice, because it was the only place where you could get one. They did not subject us to the rituals of any faith, nor did we go to any church. The only concession was a Christmas tree and the gifts under it. It was so obvious that no one ever even talked about it.

But we were raised by Nanny. Nanny, like probably all nannies, was very pious. So, she took me to church with her, and not only on Sundays, but whenever she had a moment to spare. Of course, no one knew about it. No one really paid any attention.

The church, which was across the street from our house, was somber, quiet, and mysterious. Along the walls, in every chapel, was a holy picture. I would visit the church in a systematic way, chapel by chapel, and once I even created a major incident, because Nanny, deep in her prayers, didn't notice that I'd disappeared. After a long search, the vicar pulled me out from behind a painting of Saint Therese of the Infant Jesus.[17] This saint was my ideal. I would stare at her face with adoration and worship. I admired the roses that looked alive in her hands.

In the church you could buy Lives of the Saints. The price was fixed, so you just put the money into a wooden receptacle. No one checked; they counted on the honesty of the believers. I already had at home a large collection of these Lives of the Saints and pictures with their images by the time my parents decided that I was old enough to get a weekly allowance. For a few days, Nanny and I held discussions on what to spend such an unexpected amount of money. Finally, the decision was made. It was to be a Bible, displayed in the window of a small shop on our street that sold religious goods. The book was small, bound in leather, with a gold cross and leaf embossed on the cover. From that day on, whenever I passed the store, I stopped to look at the Bible.

---

17   Thérèse of Lisieux (1873–1897), a French Carmelite nun revered for her piety; canonized in 1925 by Pope Pius XI.

After many weeks of collecting (all this time I did not buy myself a single lollipop), I had the necessary amount.

We bought the Bible. I don't know if Nanny read it. I, being seven, contented myself with taking it out from the drawer and tracing the cross and leaf on the cover with my finger. Of course, my parents knew absolutely nothing about it. Not that I hid my religious interest from them; it just never came up.

In summer, my brother and I went to the countryside. Our Łódź grandma was gone, but a new brother had appeared instead. We had gone to a village near Lask, which was not far from Łódź. The bus did not reach it, so at the beginning of the holidays, our landlord came for us with his wagon, and he brought us back from Lask later at the end of summer.

We lived with Nanny in the same room. There were two big, country beds that belonged to our hosts and a small, barred crib for my brother, who was too young for a big bed. He could fall from it. On the walls of our room hung portraits of the saints: one next to the other, big and small, almost all of them in gilded frames, with only a few encased in wood. Nanny told me that if I prayed in front of a saint's picture, God would hear me better than if I prayed on a carpet in front of my bed. In the prayer that she taught me, there was only one request I understood: "To You Lord, I raise my eyes, asking for health for my mom and dad." To make sure it came true, I would pronounce these words on my knees before every single painting. Nanny would sit on the bed, moving the beads on her rosary, while observing me with complete approval.

I started school. This was at the Municipal Labor School[18] opened by the socialist town council. It was an experimental school in terms of educational methods. It was coeducational, and religion classes were non-compulsory. Naturally, of course, I started to attend them. And obviously, without my parents' knowledge.

---

18 Miejska Szkoła Pracy, an experimental school established in Łódź in 1923. The school operated on the principles of problem-based learning and team teaching with classes broken up into groups of four or five students.

The lessons were given by a Sister of Charity. She was young and looked very pretty in her long gray dress and cap with a white bar. At every lesson, she would give us small pictures of the saints, which became the object of constant trading. I remember that for one Saint Therese, I had to give three other saints. After a few lessons, I already had a small collection, and, like everybody else, I was looking forward to new religion lessons and new pictures.

The next lesson, however, turned out to be unlike the others for me. The sister came with a small packet of pictures in her hand and immediately turned towards me.

"I'm sorry, Alinka, but you can't stay for the lesson. I didn't know that you are a little Jewish girl."

Everybody looked at me. I was stunned; my cheeks were burning.

"You have to leave," the sister repeated gently.

I got up and moved towards the door, accompanied by a deathly silence.

At home, nobody said anything. I did not even tell Nanny about it.

A few days later, the whole issue resurfaced once again, this time in a different form. There was a Scouts club[19] at the school. They also organized a Cubs pack. The meetings were run by older Girl Scouts, dressed in gray uniforms. Our entire class signed up for the Cubs. We dreamed of the days when we would get our scarves.

Two days before the big day that we all awaited with growing tension, our team leader approached me in the school restroom during recess.

"Wait, Alinka," she said, "I must tell you something very unpleasant... You can't join the Cubs. To belong to the Cubs, you have to be a Catholic, go to church, and receive your first communion. And you're a little Jewish girl."

This broke the dam. It was beyond my powers. I went back home, took the Bible out, and threw it into the stove where the lunch was

---

19 Związek Harcerstwa Polskiego, ZHP (Polish scouting and guiding organization) established in 1918. Members of the girl guides would take an active part in the Polish resistance during the Second World War, employed as nurses, messengers, and munition carriers.

being prepared. It failed to catch fire for a long time. It started to burn when Nanny came into the kitchen. I ran away, sat on the stairs, and waited for my father.

He said only, "Don't worry, I'll sign you up for another scout movement."

He never did. I didn't know why. Did he forget? Was there no other scout movement?

Did he only want to cheer me up?

That was the end of it.

Aunt Klara

My mother went away for a long time, and for reasons I couldn't understand, they sent me to Aunt Klara. Nanny stayed at home with my little brother.

Aunt Klara[20] and Uncle Ignaś[21] lived not far from us, but everything there was different: the rooms were filled with modern furniture and the floors covered with colorful kilims,[22] woven by my aunt herself. I got my own room with a bed, a small desk, and a bookshelf for my toys and schoolbooks, but all this seemed ugly and foreign to me. I could barely restrain myself from spilling ink on the lovely bed or making a hole in the airy curtain that had white polka dots.

My mother was beautiful. Everybody said so. Aunt Klara was very ugly. She had a flat, pale, expressionless face, which, even when she was smiling, did not become any more charming. She was a doctor but spent most of her days at home. She was very ill. She had high blood pressure and a weak heart. She had to take various medications all the time. So, it was even more peculiar that she would take it upon herself to take care of me.

---

20   Klara Elżbieta Margolis née Blumenfeld (?–1965).
21   Ignacy Margolis (1893–1940?).
22   A flat tapestry-woven carpet or rug common in Middle Eastern and Balkan countries.

Uncle Ignaś was my father's brother. He was a robust, handsome man, and from the first glance you could see that he was good and gentle. He was an ophthalmologist at the military hospital and often wore a captain's uniform. He loved his sickly wife very much, and the whole household functioned in such a way as to make her life as good and easy as possible.

The only real tragedy in my uncle and aunt's life was that they couldn't have children. Aunt was too sick to risk the dangers of pregnancy and labor. When I appeared in their home, she bestowed on me all her unfulfilled maternal needs.

At home, Nanny would take me every morning to the tram stop, and then I would continue the rest of the way to school on my own. There were usually many girls from my class on the tram. We had a lot of fun, giggling all the way, and this was one of the best parts of the day. My aunt, however, would get on the tram with me, then she would get off in front of the school and take me by the hand to its very door. I could have died of shame in front of my classmates.

When I came back from school, I had to take off my uniform, get into the bathtub, wash properly, and put on a clean, pretty dress — every day a different one. I fought like a lioness: "You want to turn me into a princess!" I would yell, crying my heart out. I was ashamed to go down to the courtyard where other children had marvelous fun.

When visitors came, Aunt would dress me in a black velvet or taffeta dress (the one in taffeta had lovely little roses around the neck), white socks, and black patent leather shoes. I would come out to greet the guests holding my aunt's hand and hear them say what a pretty girl I was and what unusual eyes I had. ("No wonder, a child of such a beautiful mother!") Only why was I so thin? All this time, every day, I was forced to have oatmeal for breakfast. (The rolls prepared for school I would toss behind the stove, and I would already be gone from the house by the time they were discovered.)

I would have probably been very unhappy, if not for my uncle. He would come home from work, sit in his armchair, put me on his lap—no one ever did this at home—and tell me, minute by minute, what had happened at his hospital. He would mostly talk about the children, because there were both adults and children in that hospital. I knew all those children by name; I knew who stuck a wire in his eye, who had an inflammation, and whose sight they'd managed to save through surgery.

On Sundays, I went home to visit. My father was usually absent because of some meetings. Nanny would kiss me warmly and ask if I remembered to say my prayers, but I could see clearly that all she really cared about was my brother. This was becoming more and more obvious over time.

After I returned home for good, my aunt decided to take the risk and have a child. It seems that my presence showed her that this was the most important thing in her life.

Haneczka was born through C-section and was a healthy baby. She immediately became the most important person in their home, the purpose of their lives, a source of joy and constant happiness. My aunt became prettier. She still took her medication, but her illness was almost never mentioned.

Haneczka was a normal and cute child, and most importantly, she was never sick. In the photographs from those days, you can see a nicely dressed blond girl with short hair and a big white bow pinned on top of her head, wearing white knee socks and, of course, patent leather shoes.

The war started when Haneczka was four. Uncle left with the army for the front. A few weeks later we got news that he was somewhere to the east, over the river Bug. Aunt Klara did not hesitate for a moment and followed him with their child. They met, and their subsequent fate was like that of many others. The Russians took Rovne, and most Poles were sent somewhere deep inside Russia. Uncle and Aunt, along with Haneczka, ended up in a remote village in Siberia.

Always frail and sick, Aunt Klara now fought for food, cut wood, did laundry, kept the stove burning, and, of course, took care of Haneczka. Haneczka caught scarlet fever during the epidemic, but luckily she got better and needed only a lot of bed rest.

Uncle Ignaś was the only doctor for a vast area of Siberia and was constantly called upon to visit the sick. He traveled by sled from village to village, treating people. Sometimes he was gone for several days, sometimes for several weeks.

Once, when he arrived at some village a day or two from home late at night, somebody said,

"They say a doctor's child died not far from here."

He traveled back day and night, stopping only to let the horse catch its breath.

Haneczka had died in Aunt Klara's arms as she carried her from a chair to the bed. Such sudden deaths can happen after scarlet fever.

Soon after, Uncle Ignaś died as well, supposedly of brain fever, but people said he could not endure Haneczka's death.

In 1945, I got a note summoning me to Lublin. I was greeted at the military headquarters by Aunt Klara wearing the uniform of a colonel in the First Polish Army.

Nicole

One day, during the Christmas holidays, we received a visit from our little French cousin, Nicole. This was the last holiday before the war, but we didn't know it yet. Her parents (the youngest brother of my mother and the youngest sister of my father) left for France because Jews had no access to higher education in Poland. My uncle became an engineer, building roads and bridges. My aunt bore children.

For a few years they did all right, living in the half-Polish mining village of Bethune. But work was harder and harder to find, and, finally, my unemployed uncle could no longer support his family. So, they sent their two young daughters to Poland. The older one went to an aunt in Warsaw; the younger one, Nicole, came to us.

Nicole was a tiny five-year-old girl with short dark hair and black eyes that reflected every spark in the universe. All five-year-old girls are nice and charming, but Nicole was the epitome of charm. For her birthday, which somehow came very soon, my mother bought her a short navy-colored woolen dress, full circle, with a letter N embroidered on it in shiny red thread. Wearing this dress, Nicole looked like a real-life doll straight out of a box.

Our spacious apartment suddenly became full of joy. Nicole chattered all the time, unconcerned that no one understood her, would skip around on one leg, and then turn to snuggle against somebody's hand.

She was sent to preschool, where, of course, nobody spoke French. The very first day, when she came back home, she stood in the middle of the room and, laughing all the time, said with her rolling French rrrrrr, *"Mademoiselle de kozel de baranie nóżki!"*[23]

It became a saying in our home. Even today, when I meet Nicole, now a renowned lawyer, I can barely refrain from saying again, *Mademoiselle de kozel de baranie nóżki.*

Nanny worshiped Nicole and allowed her anything, but surprisingly, I wasn't even jealous. My father spoiled her the most. Whenever he was home, she would follow his every step. When he was reading, she would wait quietly until he stopped and looked at her. When he received patients, she would stand in front of his office, and he would open the door between patients and wink at her mischievously. When he would take his half-hour nap after lunch—and nobody was allowed to disturb him—Nicole would climb onto his sofa, snuggle under his arm, and soon fall asleep with him.

At some point, it became an issue that Nicole was not included in the *Reading Primer*. Mr. Falski came to visit and stated that it was indeed an injustice, since I was there and so was Olek, and Nicole wasn't, but since the *Primer* was already printed, there was not much we could do about it. But in the end, we found a solution.

At the very beginning of the *Primer*, on the fourth or fifth page, Ola appears. There is already *Ala* and *Ala's* dog *As,* and right next to it, *Ala and Ola.* So, Mr. Falski took a thick pencil and in front of *Ola* added *Nic*, then changed the final *a* to an *e*. And it became *Nicole.* If you didn't

---

23   It is a silly phrase in fake French meaning "Mademoiselle de goat de sheep's little feet."

know already, you wouldn't even notice the correction. And certainly, no one would guess that it had been made by the author himself.

Unfortunately, this copy of the *Primer* burned during the Warsaw Uprising.

At the end of July, we received a letter from my aunt. She was coming to Poland to get the children. "There is going to be a war," she wrote. Nobody believed her—how was it possible? But before there was time to reply, my aunt appeared on our doorstep. She was very ugly, with hands worn by work.

An argument erupted immediately. Father yelled that a child was not a bundle that could be thrown from place to place, that Aunt had no right to take Nicole away from the best conditions available to her, only to return her to French poverty and misery. My aunt sobbed. My father, her oldest brother, had been like a father to her since their father's death. Mama stood at the window, pale and silent, and we, as usual, were watching through a keyhole.

A few days later, we accompanied them to the station. Nicole tried to pull away from her mother, clinging tightly to my father. He took her in his arms; she hugged his neck and snuggled.

I saw it. Tears ran down my father's face.

The train moved. We stayed motionless.

A month later, the Germans took Łódź.

Two months later, they executed my father.

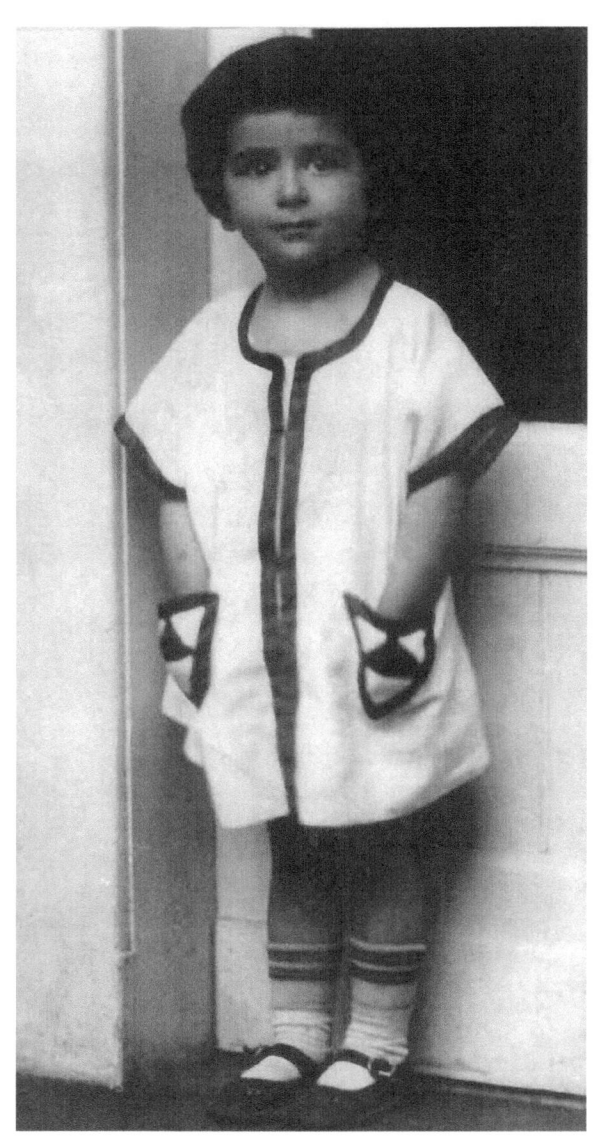

1. Three-year-old Alina, Łódź, 1925

2. Alina age 3, Brodnia near Łódź

3. Alina, Kazio Frenkiel and his sister. Brodnia near Łódź

4. Alina with her little brother Olek, 1928

5. Ala with her father. Early 1930s

6. Cover for the Polish language primer

7. This is how little Alina looks in the Reading Primer

8. Ala in Italy. photo sent to her grandmother, 1934

War

The German

It was now the first days of December 1939. The Germans had taken Łódź. Despite the war, the schools were still open. The Germans, as always happens in the first days of war, had requisitioned rooms for their officers.

Our apartment was big and beautiful. One day, when I returned from school, I heard the doorbell ring. When I opened the door, there was a German officer standing there. My heart started pounding with fear; it felt as if all my blood had drained into my heels. I was alone at home; my parents were at work, and Nanny had gone to bring my brother home from preschool.

The German came in, said something, opened one door and then another, looking inside, and then stepped into the waiting room, where the patients used to sit. There was nobody there this time of day. He sat and lit a cigarette. It was obvious that he would wait. He wasn't particularly young, but not old either; with insignia on his uniform, he was clearly an officer.

At that moment, Nanny came back, crossed herself, and called my father. He came almost immediately. He entered the waiting room, looked, and...opened his arms. The German did the same. They hugged each other for a long while.

I was speechless. Nanny crossed herself again.

Captain Hans Werner moved in with us. In civilian life, he was a teacher. It turned out that he had studied humanities in Heidelberg when my father was a medical student there. For two years they had lived in the same boarding house, some of that time as roommates. They listened to Wagner's operas together, with sheet music in their hands. They drank beer together and sang merry songs in the small student taverns.

Then they lost touch.

The German now passed his free evenings in long talks with my father.

I was devastated and ashamed of my father. All around me, people walked with their heads lowered, looking morbid, sad, and anxious. Meanwhile, my father, the highest authority in my life, was entertaining a German—the enemy of our nation, the perpetrator of a horrible war—as if he were his close friend.

On November 11th, National Independence Day in Poland, a letter with official stamps arrived. My father was summoned to the Gestapo. Why did he go? He—a wise man, an intelligent political activist—could he not have foreseen? Was he too trusting? He went and never came back.

He left a letter saying that he could not endanger all of us and that I should be good to my brother because he was little.

That same day in the afternoon, Hans Werner said that he'd found father with other hostages in Radogoszcz, in a factory converted into a prison camp.

From then on, Werner did not stop pursuing the matter. He went to the Gestapo, he wrote letters to Berlin, he spent hours calling various places, would travel, return the following day, and then call again. He was my mother's only beacon, her only hope.

Some ten days later, the Gestapo came to get Hans Werner. I was again alone at home. He put on the jacket of his uniform and his military overcoat, turned to me, and said something I did not understand. He was calm. He left and never came back.

The Germans allowed us to bring some food to the prisoners once a day. By then we were already wearing armbands with a Star of David.

Every day, I would leave the house with a canteen. Boarding a streetcar, I would immediately remove my armband. In the street-car, I met other girls who were also carrying canteens. Once, one of them, my classmate and a close neighbor, asked quite loudly, "But you're Jewish. Why don't you have an armband?"

Some women turned away silently.

One day, there was a good German at the gatehouse to the camp. When I gave him the canteen, he stopped me and asked in Polish if I wanted to see my father. He left and, in a few minutes, returned with tata. Father was wearing a coat but no hat, even though it was a cold November day. He seemed thinner, very pale, and very tired. He looked at me without a smile and asked,

"Are you doing anything?"

"Mama tried and Mr. Werner tried, but there is nothing to be done," I answered.

He looked at me and repeated,

"Nothing to be done."

After a while, the German came to take him back.

The next day they did not accept my canteen. I never saw my father again.

And I was left with this *"Nothing can be done"* for the rest of my life.

Ajfelek—As

One autumn day, still before the war, a friend of my mother came for a visit and brought us a white hamster as a gift. She told us to take good care of him because hamsters were always brown, so this white hamster was a rarity. She brought him in a cage and said people were laughing at her, thinking she was carrying a mouse in that cage.

We made a terrarium for the hamster. It really was just a regular fish tank, but we put some big and small pebbles at the bottom so he could have caves and hideouts, and we hung a stick on a rope that moved like a real swing. Since the hamster came from Paris, we named him Ayfelek after the Eiffel Tower. My little brother didn't know what the Eiffel Tower was, but it didn't matter.

And then one day, Mr. Falski came to visit. Of course, we immediately showed him Ayfelek. Mr. Falski confirmed what we'd already known: that Ayfelek was very cute. Then he frowned and asked,

"So, what did you say his name was? Ayfelek? What Ayfelek? Don't you remember that there is Ala and As in the *Primer*? So, what's with Ayfelek?"

There was no other way. Ayfelek got a second name, and now he was called Ayfelek-As. It was still a pretty name, and Mr. Falski was happy.

Ayfelek-As was cute, but we loved him mostly because he was very funny. He would stand on his hind legs, raise his little head and sway left and right. He would also swing on our stick and never fall off.

After some time, we let him leave the terrarium, and he would run and thoroughly explore the entire house. He also loved to climb up my brother's shirt sleeve, stay there for a long time, and then leave through the open collar. Sometimes, the two of them would spend a whole day like that, and later they became really inseparable. It made me terribly jealous.

One day, disaster struck. Ayfelek-As got into the pantry and ate rat poison that was sprinkled in a corner. At lunchtime, we found him lying stiff on the kitchen floor, his little legs straightened. My brother, as was usual for him, burst out crying, but this time I was also in tears. We left our unfinished lunch, and, in a few minutes, we drove with my mother to the veterinarian. The vet made a very serious face but said that he would try and told my brother to stop crying because it was distracting. And he gave Ayfelek-As a real enema.

Later, no one would believe us.

We left Ayfelek-As at the vet's. He lived. The next day he came back home. It was a great family celebration. Even my father participated.

At the end of spring, Ayfelek-As went crazy. He would run madly around the floor, and we had to be very careful not to step on him. In his terrarium, he was constantly climbing the smooth glass walls, as if trying to conquer that icy mountain. He performed such acrobatics under my brother's shirt that we could see him moving like a small ball - first up and down, then to the front and then the back.

We went to the vet.

It turned out that Ayfelek-As was a female and simply wanted to have children!!!

We had to give Ayfelek-As to the zoo. They found him (her) a partner there, but there was no other white hamster in the whole town - something we'd always known anyway. So, the future father was brown, and the little hamsters turned out...pink!!!

All this gained us the right to enter the zoo at any time by a back entrance. This instantly raised my status at school. All my classmates now tried buttering me up so they could also go with me to the zoo by the back door.

When the little hamsters grew up, we took Ayfelek-As home. It was a triumphal return!

And then the war started.

When they took our father, mama would not stop looking for him. She was very busy. People were saying that there would be a ghetto in town at any moment. So, mama decided to send us to our aunt in Warsaw. She couldn't go herself, she didn't want to leave—she was waiting for father.

At that time, you had to travel to the General Government[24] part of Poland by crossing the border illegally. My brother and I went in a taxi. There were three adults in the car, along with the taxi driver and the two of us. One lady was dark and thin and didn't take much space. The other was blond, fat, and wore a thick fur jacket that made her even fatter. The third passenger, a man, had a huge backpack which he wouldn't put down even for a moment. At the rear window, behind the back seat, we put a cage with Ayfelek-As. It was crowded, especially because the cab was filled with things up to the roof—so much so that even the rear window was obscured.

---

24   General Government: the name given to the German-occupied part of Poland, minus those sections annexed to the Reich. Łódź had been annexed to Germany as part of new Germany territory of Wartheland and was renamed Litzmannstadt.

Mama followed us right to the highway, and then she went back. We couldn't even see her through the rear window, but still I somehow knew that she would be walking slowly, slowly, with her lips pressed tight, and maybe she would even be crying, just as I had seen her do once before. Or maybe she wouldn't even be able to walk anymore, the tears blinding her eyes. That's how I still saw her, although we had already gone very far.

The driver stopped and said that we would soon reach the border, so we had to get our belongings. We were supposed to cross the border on foot, and another cab would be waiting for us on the other side. It was getting dark. We started to unload the luggage. Next to the cab a mountain was growing, bigger than the cab itself, then as big as two cabs, and finally the rear window was cleared.

Ayfelek-As's cage was empty!!!

Panicked, we started to look for him - in the car, behind the seats, under the wheel, under the seat covers. Ajfelek-As had disappeared. Our co-passengers initially helped us search but then started to get nervous. Time was passing, it was getting darker. Somewhere in the forest were German patrols. My brother burst out crying and was making a lot of noise. For a moment, I was afraid that they would strangle him. They put two big hands on his mouth and nose. I bit those hands. They released him.

The hamster was gone. Suddenly, I noticed a field of carrots nearby. I ran to grab a carrot and then put it on the floor of the cab. I waited; all tense—nothing! The driver said angrily,

"You're coming with everybody else, or I'm leaving you here, damn brats!"

I was swallowing tears. Olek was sobbing. We couldn't leave Ayfelek-As. He was a part of our home; he was all we had left. We did not have our mama or tata with us anymore. And we loved him. But how could we stay alone in the forest this dark night? What would we do with ourselves and our suitcases? And what would mama say?!

The driver stood above me,

"So, what is it, young lady, are you staying?"

At this very moment, the fat blond in the fur jacket bent down to reach under the front seat, where she'd hidden her purse with her money. Suddenly, she screamed and grabbed her finger. There were two narrow white marks on it. Ajfelek-As, half-dead with fear, was hiding between the springs of the front seat and, scared by a strange hand, had bitten into it with his two sharp little teeth.

It was getting really dark. I put Ayfelek-As in the pocket of my coat and held the pocket closed with all my strength.

After we moved in with my aunt on Mokotowska Street,[25] our duty, as that of all other children, was to collect the bits of coal that fell off the shaky coal wagons. One day, Ayfelek-As got lost. We looked for him until dusk and again the next day. He'd been run over by a wagon wheel.

---

25 A major street in Warsaw's Śródmieście or central district leading to the district of Mokotów.

The Ghetto

Olek

My brother was born exactly on my birthday. Tata walked into the room and said, "So, for your birthday gift you've got a brother. He'll be coming here soon."

Since no one had prepared me for it and I had no idea anything like this was going to happen—mama was getting treatments for her asthma, so she was away for a few months—I was more surprised than happy with the news. Besides, I was expecting a real gift.

Then mama came home and we were supposed to choose a name for my brother. But it turned out that there was no choice whatsoever, because in Mr. Falski's *Primer* there was an Ala and an Olek, so it was obvious that my brother had to be named Olek.

In the *Primer* there was also Zosia, but mama said that she would not have any more children and, as it turned out later, she was absolutely right, because she probably wouldn't have been able to save more than two from the Warsaw ghetto.

Olek immediately assumed a major position in the life of our family, mostly because of Nanny, who took exclusive care of him from day one. It seemed that the only thing that still connected her to me was making sure that I brushed my teeth every day — with toothpaste in the evening but only with a brush in the morning to prevent plaque. I suppose that I must have been jealous, but it soon became obvious that Olek did not have much time to profit from his privileged childhood. He was barely grown when the war started, tata got arrested, and we went to live with our aunt in Warsaw and life separated us from mama. When she finally joined us in Warsaw, we had to move to the ghetto.

The three of us moved into a small railroad flat on Ceglana Street.[26] Mrs. Franka who, with her little son Wojtuś, lived next door, had to cross our room to get to hers. Mrs. Franka was a teacher of Polish, about forty years of age. She was plump, but attractive. In the beginning she laughed a lot, and even later, during the worst days, she always took care of her appearance: she would darken her eyebrows with a pencil and put light rosy blush on her cheeks. Despite her age, she was quite a coquette, flirting with everyone, no matter what age and gender. Besides us, there was nobody else in the apartment.

Mrs. Franka's little son, Wojtuś, who was four years old, went to a "preschool." This "preschool" was in the building next door, on the fourth floor. It was attended sometimes by a few, sometimes by a dozen small children. Two frail old ladies took care of the children, giving them something to drink. They had no food. These ladies were barely alive. One was almost blind and sometimes, walking across the room, she would bump into a child standing in the middle. The other one was crippled and walked with a heavy orthopedic shoe on her foot. It made her movements very difficult. Sometimes she would smash a child's foot with this shoe and the child would burst into short, unanswered sobs.

Soon, I moved to the dormitory of the nursing school while mama stayed alone with Olek. Olek was eight at that time. When mama would leave for work at the hospital, Olek would go downstairs to a so-called "corner," where some older girls took care of the children. Such "corners" were then in almost every courtyard, full of children who were left alone during the day. The courtyards were small, very dirty, full of dust and garbage, and populated by squatters—fam-

---

26   A small side street in the southern part of the Warsaw ghetto, not far from the Tö-
      bbens textile factory.

ilies squeezed into the Warsaw ghetto from Germany, Hungary, and many other countries. But the children liked their "corners." They let older kids organize various games and activities, and they even sang songs. One song, which went "Train cars, green train cars...," was really quite innocent but later seemed ominous. But luckily, the children didn't form any associations yet.

My brother, since the moment he'd taken his first steps at the age of eighteen months, always turned to look at little girls. It was very funny and friends used to say that he would grow up to become a real Don Juan! So, it was not surprising that in the "corner" at Ceglana, he immediately spotted a couple of girls. It was a bit complicated though, because the girls were twins. On top of it, they were identical twins, which really made his choice difficult. Anyway, those twins became an integral part of my memories of Ceglana.

One day, Mrs. Franka discovered that her antique locket, with an engraved portrait of her great grandmother, was lost. It was not only a cherished family heirloom. It was also made of platinum, with seed pearls around her great-grandmother's likeness. All this on a platinum chain, also with seed pearls woven into it. So, the locket was lost. We searched both rooms dozens of times, we looked into all the boxes, closets, and nooks... Nothing. It had disappeared. Mrs. Franka was very easygoing, but it was obvious that she was upset because, on top of everything, she considered this locket her good luck charm, believing that her distant great grandmother was protecting her from evil.

Sometime later, maybe two weeks, I came home and since nobody was there, I went downstairs to look for Olek in his "corner." In a corner of the courtyard, close to the wall, there was a small group of little girls. They had their backs to me and stood so tightly that you couldn't squeeze a pin between them. They were bending over something, so I could see only the tops of their heads. I recognized the twins who stood in the middle. I came closer and pushed my way inside the circle.

One of the twins held Mrs. Franka's locket in her slightly open palm. The other held the chain with pearls.

This was a complicated matter.

The ethical problem—my eight-year-old brother was a thief.

The tactical problem—tell mama? She had enough troubles without it. Tell Mrs. Franka? Our relations were so good that I dreaded their possible deterioration.

And there were attenuating circumstances: Olek was in love with the twins and wanted to give them the most beautiful thing in the world. Olek didn't know the material value of the locket. Olek hadn't yet acquired faith in the magical power of things.

The locket was returned to Mrs. Franka. But it didn't help her at all. Four days after she celebrated its recovery, still beaming with happiness, the Germans came and took both of the women who ran Wojtuś's "preschool" away—along with all the children.

After this happened, mama decided to send Olek out of the ghetto. The telephones still worked and communication with the Aryan side was possible. Moreover, the passage through the courtyard on Leszno Street was then still relatively safe. The courtyard of the six-story building could be accessed both from the ghetto on Chłodna Street and from the Polish side on Leszno. The courtyard and building were always very busy, with various proceedings taking place in many rooms. People crowded the vast corridors, walked up and down the stairs to different floors, and got lost in the corners.

One only had to melt into the crowd, quickly remove their armband, and exit the courtyard on Leszno Street. It might have seemed simple and relatively safe, but the dangers and difficulties lurked right outside, at the exit door. That's where those guys were waiting. They looked just like everybody else, but they were vigilant, careful, and experienced in recognizing Jews. A person who'd just gotten rid of his armband and walked into the dreamed-of Aryan side barely had time to feel relief. He was instantly followed by one, two, or three guys in overcoats or plaid jackets with visor caps and scarves around their necks or, depending on the weather, wearing just flannel shirts.

These guys, called *szmalcowniks*,[27] would quickly follow you, hands in their pockets. Then, one would move on ahead, another would sidle

---

[27] From the Polish word *szmalec* meaning lard or grease, since victims had to grease their palms with money to avoid being turned over to the police.

up alongside you, sometimes even with a polite "excuse me," while the third would close in on you from behind, almost stepping on your heels. Their steps pounded on the pavement and in the head and temples of the person being followed.

So, even if you had prepared, discussed, confirmed, and memorized an address where you could go, an address of friends or people who would accept money, this address would now become unattainable and useless. What followed depended on circumstances. After a command issued in the next doorway - "Pull down your pants!" - some men managed to pay their way out. Others were taken to the Polish police station, where you needed a lot of money, watches, or jewelry. Still others—naïve and misinformed—were taken straight to the Germans, where they were shot on the spot, which for a Jew who ran away from the ghetto was still better than the Pawiak prison.[28]

This was the road on which mama sent Olek. We never discussed afterward how she had made this decision. Being a mother was probably the worst thing in the ghetto.

Olek was small and looked younger than his eight years. He was blond and had my father's blue eyes. He had a straight little nose and didn't look like a Jewish child at all, not in any way. His greatest asset and chance for survival was that he was not circumcised. This was a result of my parents' atheistic worldview and their rejection of religious demands. It caused Olek constant medical problems—painful recurrent inflammation of the foreskin. I remember Nanny saying that the Jewish God obviously didn't like it when his commands were not respected and this was the reason for Olek's problems, which, according to her, never happened to other non-circumcised, non-Jewish boys.

It was agreed that after leaving the courtyard, Olek would turn right and then walk two blocks further along, where Nanny would be waiting for him. Every night, mama would wake Olek from a deep sleep and ask him what his new name was and which way he would

---

28   The main prison in Warsaw, built in 1835. It was taken over by the German Security Police and Security Service (SD) from October 1939 to August 1944. Some 65,000 people passed through Pawiak during the occupation, around half of whom were executed by the German and Ukrainian guards.

turn when he got out. Eventually, he would start answering her the moment she started to shake him, before he was really awake. She decided he was ready.

We walked with Olek to the courtyard, but we couldn't get inside with him. We were afraid someone would notice us. So he had to enter alone: no looking back at mama, no turning around, and especially, no crying. It was not an easy task for an eight-year-old.

And so Olek left the ghetto. He was a brave little boy. When those guys caught him a few steps from the courtyard, saying, "Come with us, little kike," and told him to get to the doorway, he was calm. He told us later that he wasn't afraid at all. Well, maybe it's even true. Anyway, after that, everything went really smoothly. For two days, Nanny hid him in her room. She had to hide him because she now worked for some people who under no circumstances should discover that she was harboring a Jewish child.

Then, Nanny took Olek to "Our Home." This was an orphanage run by Mrs. Maryna Falska.[29] Olek arrived when all the children were sitting in the cafeteria. Mrs. Falska said, "I want you to meet a new classmate. He is not just any classmate. He is Olek from the *Reading Primer*."

And this is how Olek survived the war.

The School of Nursing

On the crowded, dirty, gray, and colorless streets of the ghetto, one could sometimes see groups of girls in pink dresses, white aprons with straps, and white caps. They looked like the pink petals of flowers, maybe alpine violets, and their brightness, purity, and pastel coloring

---

29 Maria Rogowska-Falska (1877–1944), Polish teacher, pedagogue, and activist. Together with Janusz Korczak, she helped found the Nasz Dom (Our house) children's orphanage in Warsaw in 1919. Falska died of a sudden heart attack on September 7, 1944, when the Germans forced the evacuation of the orphanage to the Pruszków transit camp during the Warsaw Uprising.

made them seem like unreal beings, fairies who had appeared from unknown lands.

These girls were students at the school of nursing.[30] The school, not just any nursing school, but the "American" one, was moved to the ghetto with the Jewish hospital from Czyste Street. The students lived in the dorm, took classes at the school, and practiced in the hospitals that still existed. Every day they walked from school to the hospitals and back.

This was a three-year school, which meant it had three levels. On graduation, you received a diploma, one of the most respected in the world. Before the ghetto, the school accepted only high school graduates through a process of strict selection aimed at finding only those candidates who had a real vocation.

When the school moved to the ghetto and got an entire two-story building at 2 Mariańska Street, it immediately became clear that its students would have a special chance, that they would be protected— who knows—they might even be safe. Everybody tried to get their daughters into the school. People falsified birth certificates or forged high school diplomas. Often, especially in the first year, the girls were thirteen or fourteen. The director certainly knew, but it was never mentioned. Only three instructors were real nurses, recent graduates of the school, who had moved with it to the ghetto. Other girls, almost to the very end that awaited them at the Umschlagplatz,[31] were childish and not very serious.

Mama managed to place me in the school. She was a doctor, a single mother with two children, and also a known social activist.

So, I moved to the dorm. The building at Mariańska Street was big and comfortable. You could forget that you were in the ghetto there.

---

30   Żydowska Szkoła Pielęgniarstwa (Jewish nursing school), established in 1923, with assistance of the American Jewish Joint Distribution Committee, as part of the Jewish Hospital on Czyste Street in Warsaw. In the ghetto, the school was managed by Luba Blum-Bielicka (1905–1973), the wife of Bund activist and ghetto fighter Abrasza Blum (1905–1943).

31   German: collection point or loading point. Term given to the holding areas adjacent to railway stations in German-occupied Poland for deportation to the Nazi death camps.

There was an entrance on the ground floor with a student from the first grade always on duty. Next to it was the director's office and a room where she lived with her husband and two children. In the hall, at the place of honor, very visible, was a portrait of Florence Nightingale—the great nurse—who was to be our role model from now on.

To enter the school, you had to ring a bell and the student on duty would open the door. The door was covered with a thick curtain and after you stepped behind it, you had the impression that the outside world was a different world altogether and that you were separated from it by this curtain, this silent hall, this perfect order. Even the hunger there seemed like a different hunger.

The director was a big, stocky woman, always dressed in a white coat with long sleeves and a big, navy blue cape with red lining. She wore a big white bonnet on her tightly pulled-back hair, a bonnet bigger than all the others, with a broad black velvet stripe, broader than on all other bonnets. From day one, the director introduced an iron regime, exactly like the one that ruled the school from its very beginning. She simply did not accept the fact that the school was now in the ghetto.

Her husband was a small, thin, slightly stooped man who skittered along the hall as fast as he could without raising his eyes from the floor. He seemed as if he were constantly apologizing for his very existence. We were not particularly surprised. It must not have been easy being married to the director. Much later, after he had already perished, I learned that he was a very important person in the ghetto underground organization.

On the ground floor, beside the director's office, there was also an auditorium and a room for nursing practice, performed on a doll the size of a four-year-old child. The doll lay on a hospital bed, and each of us, from the first, earliest year, had to make this bed numerous times a day, performing identical movements, folding the corners and pulling the sheet to make it as smooth as an ice-skating rink. We practiced sub-dermal and intramuscular injections (the nurses were not allowed to make intravenous injections) on the doll as well as IVs, enemas, and compresses. We also rubbed her back with vinegar and dusted her with talc.

The lectures were given by doctors from the hospitals. They taught us all medical subjects very meticulously. For some of us it was so unexpected that it seemed hardly real. We had notebooks, we copied lectures, and we received grades. There was a whole lecture on lice. Lice were a plague in the ghetto. Posters on the walls advised you to "avoid filth, always be clean, filth brings lice and typhoid fever."[32] One doctor told us that lice liked "warmth, darkness, and dampness," so there were always many of them under skull caps. That's where we had to look for them.

The doctor who taught us surgery was our idol. He was young, slim, with dark hair, beautiful blue eyes, and a charming smile. From the youngest to the oldest, we were all in love with him, dreaming about an acute case of appendicitis, only to have him perform the operation.

The bedrooms were on the upper floors—with the second year on the first floor and the third year, the smallest year—on the second. Every bedroom had ten to twelve beds placed in rows, each with a blanket, a pillow, and clean, white linen. The beds had to be made to perfection, without the smallest crease. Every day, around ten in the morning, one of the instructors came for inspection, and those beds that were not perfect had to be made again. We were not allowed to enter the bedrooms during the day, while at night complete silence was imposed from eight pm on. Since we were rather childish and our behavior quite deficient, the instructor often had to summon the director for help.

Each of us, back then, still had a family in town, so after the nighttime curfew, we would secretly sneak out of the school, arranging the blanket to look as if someone were sleeping.

At the very bottom of the building, in the basement, there was a kitchen and a dining room. In the dining room there were tables for four, each covered with a small oilcloth. Every day, at six in the morning, two students on duty went to the dining room to set the tables: four plates and four teacups on each. Very soon, after a few weeks of school, there was only one eighth and then one sixteenth of a loaf

---

32   A rhyming couplet in Polish: *Unikaj brudu, bądź zawsze czysty/Brudy wesz rodzą, wiesz— tyfus plamisty.*

of bread on each plate. This had to be enough for the entire day. But it was always served on a white plate.

At some point we noticed that when we came down in the morning, the bread was already missing from a few of the plates. This was very dangerous. It meant that some students had nothing to eat for the whole day. We tried to keep guard, but nothing helped. Then, one after the other, we were called to the director's office. No one was punished, but the bread stopped disappearing.

Half of the day we spent in hospitals. One of them, a children's hospital, was on Śliska Street, very close to the school; another, for adults, was on Leszno. Later, we also worked in the hospital on Stawki Street.

We walked to work in our uniforms. They were really pretty: pink and white striped dresses and white aprons with straps crossed at the back. The dresses had tiny short sleeves with small white cuffs and white collars. The collars remained starched at the school almost to the end of the ghetto. We wore light white bonnets on our heads, held in place with elastic at the back. Upon finishing the second year, we were supposed to get a black velvet ribbon sewn across our bonnets. Outside, we wore wide navy blue capes. The students' capes were lined with navy blue fabric, the instructors' with blue, and the director's with red.

No wonder that for a long time we seemed untouchable. The Jewish policemen did not bother us, and if it happened that one of us was taken by the Germans to the Umschlagplatz, there was always a way to get her out. Of course, this did not last until the end.

In those days, when the hospital was still a hospital and the patients still had beds, we worked three shifts: morning, afternoon, and night. There was always more of us than regular nurses, so we provided the sick with "luxury" care. The director would come three times a day for inspection to supervise her students' work. We had it worse at Śliska because it was so close to the school that she could drop in more often.

We nicknamed her the "Cow," and when she was noticed in the hospital, our hissing whispers, "Cowwww," announced her arrival. It meant that we had to hurriedly smooth the sheets and wipe the windowsills with a dust cloth so that she could not detect even a trace of dirt on a finger of her white glove, worn especially for this purpose.

We were really young and stupid, so we composed silly couplets and sung them in such a way that she would hear. After each of many stanzas there would be the refrain: "We have such a headache now, from three times per day of Cow, and that's what Śliska is!"

It's shameful to admit, but in summer, after a shift in the hospital on Stawki, we would climb to the top floor and sunbathe on a terrace there, rubbing ourselves with cocoa butter from the suppositories that none of our patients needed anyway. They all had diarrhea.

This would all take place when corpses covered with paper lay on the streets beyond the hospital windows, when starving boys would grab any food they'd notice from passersby and run away stuffing it into their mouths, when there were shots along the ghetto walls, and the cemeteries couldn't cope with burying all the arriving dead.

The director of the school has been dead for a long time now, so we can never know if the ironfisted discipline she imposed on her students in the Warsaw ghetto until the last moment was her own kind of resistance movement, her own private Jewish Combat Organization, or her own credo of faith in the ideals that she'd cherished all her life and which were personified by Florence Nightingale, whose portrait hung on the school's wall.

Or maybe it was just proof of her lack of imagination.

"Oh, that's just like the Cow," the girls in pink dresses might have said if they'd avoided going to the gas chambers.

My Dorm Room

There were a lot of pretty girls in our school at the beginning. We had not yet wasted away, and the dormitory provided a screen, a cover, an escape from everything that was experienced by the other inhabitants of the ghetto.

Today, it is hard for me to realize that we were all Jewish. Krysia, Zenka, Dorka, and the other girls in my dorm room had no typically Jewish characteristics in their looks, behavior, or in what occupied their minds at that time.

There were so many pretty girls in our school, but, in our opinion, the prettiest ones were in our room.

Krysia, whose father was chief of surgery at the hospital on Leszno Street, was a redhead with freckles on her nose and a charming smile that disarmed not only her instructors but even the director herself.

Krysia had a younger sister whom her parents had sent to the Aryan side, but no one knew what had happened to her there. Krysia often cried at night.

Zenia had a round face, long chestnut hair and, for as long as I knew her, joyful eyes that laughed even when she seemed absolutely serious. She plaited her hair into a long, thick braid that reached almost to her waist, which she wrapped tightly around her head so it created a kind of turban. From under this turban, small locks of hair sneaked out onto her forehead, forming unintentional curls. Every evening, she sat on her bed and spent a long time combing her hair, chattering nonstop about anything that came to her mind.

Zenia wanted to become an archeologist in Egypt and openly regarded her stay at the school of nursing in the Warsaw ghetto as a misunderstanding that was just a temporary nightmare.

Most astonishingly, Zenia did become an archeologist in Egypt.

Felka was a light blond and her unruly long hair was very difficult to keep under her bonnet, as required by the instructors. Felka was a very practical and direct girl. She never participated in our pranks and decided that, since we had the good/bad luck to be locked in a dorm, we should just accept it.

Felka's father was a well-known Warsaw tailor, and her dream was to become a model and present beautiful clothes at fashion shows.

Next to me slept Dorka. She looked more serious than the rest of us. One can even say that she looked like a mature high school graduate, like the only one who really had the right to be here in our school. It was not so in reality. She was fourteen, but she was tall, big, moved slowly and quietly, spoke slowly and sparely, and always very sensibly. She had dark hair and dark eyes but did not look Jewish at all.

Among all the girls in our room, only Dorka really wanted to become a nurse.

Across the room was Fredi's bed. Fredi was a niece of Doctor Braude-Hellerowa,[33] who was chief physician at the Bersohn and Bauman Children's Hospital[34] on Śliska Street. Fredi was slim and very delicate; her black Jewish eyes attracted attention with their sad expression. Nobody could remain unaffected by their look.

After a few months, Fredi fell seriously ill. They suspected paralysis connected to polio or something similar: one after another, new groups of her muscles would stop functioning. Dr. Braude-Hellerowa managed to smuggle in some consultants from the Aryan side via the courtyard on Leszno Street, but even they couldn't help. We nursed Fredi day and night, with our hearts in our throats, feeling totally helpless. In the end, the paralysis attacked her respiratory muscles, and Fredi suffocated a few months before the "resettlement" action began in the ghetto.

The absolutely prettiest girl in the whole school was Ewa. She was so beautiful that you couldn't take your eyes off her. She was tall, a head taller than the rest of us, with very short, black curly hair and clear blue-green eyes. She had a light, almost powdery complexion and a rosy blush on her slightly high cheekbones. She looked like a beautiful and exquisite illustration. When she walked through the streets in her white-pink uniform, one would think that she was some American movie star who alighted in the middle of the ghetto from a helicopter.

Ewa, like me, came to Warsaw from Łódź. She'd attended the same municipal labor school, only a year or two ahead of me. We knew each other well since we were neighbors and had taken the same tram to

---

33   Dr. Anna Braude-Hellerowa (1888–1943), Polish-Jewish pediatrician and activist. Braude-Hellerowa helped cofound the Towarzystwo Przyjaciół Dzieci (Society of Friends of Children) in 1919. She was instrumental in the reopening of Bersohn and Bauman Children's Hospital in 1930 and directed it during the time of the Warsaw ghetto. Braude-Hellerowa perished during the Warsaw ghetto uprising.

34   The Bersohn and Bauman Children's Hospital (Szpital Dziecięcy Bersohnów i Baumanów) was established in 1878 on the initiative of two Polish-Jewish families, the Bershons and the Baumans. It was located almost its entire existence at 51 Śliska Street, with a further branch at 80/82 Leszno Street during the ghetto. In August 1942, the hospital was moved to 6/8 Stawki Street, near the Umschlagplatz. On September 11, 1942, most of the remaining staff and patients were transported to Treblinka.

school, which was at the other end of town. I knew her mother, a tall, very attractive woman whom Ewa very much resembled, and her father, who was short and shy—the unassuming husband of a beautiful wife. Her little brother was exactly the same age as my brother, Olek. That's why for me, Ewa was not just a regular classmate from the school of nursing but seemed like a part of my family, a bridge to what had been before.

Red Roses

One day, the bell rang at the school's front door. There was a man there. He was holding a huge bouquet of red roses. He handed it to the girl on duty, together with a small love note, and quickly left.

The roses were for Ewa.

Everybody knows the landscape of the Warsaw ghetto: the unimaginable filth, the narrow streets full of gray, emaciated people, the heaps of unremoved garbage, and the wailing, half-naked skeletons, sometimes covered with paper, sometimes not.

Yet in this ghetto, where not one green leaf was to be found and where small children had never heard about forests, trees, or flowers, this huge bouquet of red roses appeared. Roses that were full and delicate at the same time, as only roses can be, some still in bud, others with slightly open petals, still others already blooming, lush and succulent. This bouquet of red roses was breathtaking.

From that day on, a bouquet of red roses appeared at the school every week. Each time it was brought by a different person who disappeared in an instant.

Who was sending those roses? Who was this secret admirer? It was clear that he was sending them from the Aryan side, probably via the courtyard at Leszno Street. But who was he? A rich heir of some fortune on the other side? An American diplomat? A German from the Wehrmacht? A Jewish policeman from the ghetto? A fairytale prince? We could talk of nothing else in the evenings after the instructor turned off the lights.

Ewa did not participate in our discussions. She kept to herself. This was after the first round ups, and the Germans had already taken her parents and her little brother. She was left completely alone. It had all just begun and the deportation of relatives was not yet a daily occurrence. The feeling of numbness that affected many people after the first shock of losing their loved ones hadn't hit yet.

And suddenly those roses.

Ewa, like most of us, knew no more about this whole "falling in love" thing than a walk back from school with a boy carrying your school bag. Or maybe a note that was passed during a lesson with an "I love you" written in printed letters so that the author could not be identified.

And now those roses.

Time passed. The ghetto was being liquidated. The school was going to vanish. We were leaving our cocoon and joining reality, where there was no cover. We were suddenly like everybody else.

On the last day, when there was almost no one left in the school building on Mariańska Street except for the director and a few students, another messenger appeared. He didn't bring roses. He came for Ewa.

For a long time, you could still leave the ghetto if you had money to bribe the Germans, the police, or the *szmalcowniks* on the other side.

The messenger took Ewa away. She went with him without a second thought.

What was she to do?

I lost touch with Ewa until the end of the war which, as we discovered, we had both survived in Warsaw on the Aryan side. We met again in Łódź.

The fairytale prince turned out to be just the son of some rich Jewish industrialists who, before their deaths, had managed to hide part of their fortune on the Aryan side. Some of it got to their son.

Stefan was a young man with very Semitic looks. He'd left the ghetto after the first action and went into hiding at the place where his parents had left their money. The people who hid him, thanks to this money, were able to avoid misery. They had a number of children and sick elderly parents. Stefan, like many others, had a hiding place behind a closet, which he very seldom left.

He met Ewa on the street before escaping from the ghetto. The beautiful apparition was a case of love at first sight for the lonely and mortally threatened young man. All he knew about her was that she was a student at the school and that her name was Ewa.

So, Ewa left for the Aryan side and began living with Stefan and the people to whom she was brought by his messenger. She bleached her hair and became a light blond. Since she had blue eyes and her Polish was perfect, nobody could suspect that she was Jewish.

Together with the woman who was hiding Stefan, Ewa became a street vendor. The money was gone, and the woman's husband had been caught by the Germans and sent to Germany for forced labor, so now the two of them supported Stefan, the elderly parents, and the children themselves.

Once, Ewa was stopped by the police for illegal trading. While waiting at the police station in despair, an older woman who worked there started conversing with her. She helped Ewa get back home. The woman, who really disliked the Jews because they "were the reason why Hitler invaded Poland," became Ewa's protector and friend for the rest of her life. After the war, she learned the truth and moved with Ewa to Israel.

When the Warsaw Uprising started, Ewa wasn't at home, and she couldn't make her way back. She lost track of Stefan and had no news from him. She was certain he wouldn't survive with his very Jewish looks. She loved him very much by then and thought that if she couldn't find him, it meant the world would end for her a second time.

She didn't find him.

After the war, Ewa went back to Łódź, not really knowing what for. She was a dark brunette once again, as beautiful as before, perhaps even more so now that she was mature.

An older man, almost forty, who'd lost his wife in Treblinka[35] fell head over heels in love with her. He had a nervous tic, likely because

---

35   Located in a forested area near the eponymous village northeast of Warsaw, Treblinka was the second-deadliest extermination camp run by the Germans in the Second World War and the main destination of Jewish transports from the Warsaw ghetto. An estimated 700,000–900,000 people lost their lives at Treblinka before it was closed in late 1943.

of his war experience: every few minutes, very regularly, he would sort of shake his head, or more like jerk it backward. Other than that, he was nice and good and very quickly started making money. He brought Ewa gifts, surrounded her with the protection of a man in love, but also somewhat like a father figure. Sometime later, Ewa moved in with him and they got married.

What was she to do?

A year later, Ewa got pregnant. She was maybe six months along when a red Volvo convertible stopped in front of her house. Stefan stepped out of the car. He had come for Ewa. He'd been deported by the Germans after the uprising. When the war ended, he was very sick. He started working in Germany, but he didn't want to come to her poor and in rags. No one really knew how he'd found her. The car he bought was red because he deemed it the only one worthy of her and thought that she would look more beautiful in it than Liz Taylor herself.

Two days later, Ewa told Stefan to leave.

What was she to do?

Cakes

For some time, when leaving the hospital on Śliska Street, we would see a well-dressed young man at the entrance. We didn't pay him much attention, although he looked different than other people on the street.

One day he followed us right to the school.

We joked that he seemed to have a problem deciding which of us he liked best. After a few days, he started to walk closer to Krysia. She also seemed to lag behind. Then, out of the blue, he asked her if she would like to go with him to a café.

This was a revelation for us because we had no idea that there was a café in the ghetto. After discussing the issue in our bedroom in the evening, we decided that he had invented this whole café, and in reality, it did not exist at all. But we also decided that Krysia should agree to go. She would sneak out of the dorm after the instructor left, arranging the blankets the usual way in the shape of a sleeping person.

And so she went. We waited for her, all very excited, and none of us could fall asleep, except for Fredzia, who always slept like a log.

Krysia came back sometime after midnight. She put a paper bag on the table and started taking cakes out of the bag, laughing like crazy.

He had really invited her to a café.

There really was a café in the ghetto.

There were well-dressed people in the café. They were talking; couples were embracing.

He summoned a waiter who brought a whole plate of cakes. It was so unexpected, so like a dream, a fairytale, a theater performance. How long was it since Krysia had even seen a slice of white bread? She felt lightheaded. Was she really in the ghetto?

But she immediately formed a plan: cakes for all of us!

So, while slowly munching on the cake on her plate, she sneaked a second, third, and fourth one into a bag under her cape. She kept chattering all this time to divert his attention from the cakes. He looked into her eyes and kept asking her some questions, but she didn't know what he was talking about, which was only natural because it was the first time in her life that she was alone with a young man.

And now here she was taking cake after cake out of the bag: with poppy seeds, with marmalade, with cheese, a chocolate cake, a custard babka, a slightly crumbled cream cake.

Dumbfounded, we approached the cakes on our tiptoes. Krysia stood there laughing, happy, and excited.

Then we ate the cakes, each of us in her own way:

Felka devoured hers instantly. Zenia licked hers slowly. Dorka nibbled a bit from each side. Only Fredzia, who'd just woken up, hid her cake under her pillow for her hungry father.

When the instructor came in the morning to check the beds, we had a real problem: how to hide the grease stain under Fredzia's pillow.

Krysia agreed to meet her pastry man for another date. But another date did not happen. He did not come to the hospital gate again. You could think about it in many ways, but it was best not to think about it at all.

The ghetto ended, the war ended. Krysia survived the war and moved to England. She became a doctor, worked in a hospital. She had a husband and grown children.

One day, in the summer, it was very hot. Wearing her white coat, she walked out for a moment in front of the hospital gate. Suddenly she stopped as if struck by lightning.

He stood across the street. There was no doubt, although his hair was gray and he was slightly stooped. He noticed her, stretched out his arms. She ran across the street as if she were still fifteen. He said, "You look just the same," and there were tears in his eyes.

He invited her to a café and ordered a plate of cakes. She declined. She said she didn't like cakes.

He said, "And I thought you loved them. That time, you must have eaten about a dozen."

The Shots

At that time, we lived on the fourth floor at 6 Gęsia Street. My mother worked in the "little ghetto" in the small Bersohn and Bauman Children's Hospital. During the first roundup, the "little ghetto" was closed, and its patients and personnel were deported with all the others. What was left of the hospital, including some of its patients, both children and adults, was moved to a regular building on Gęsia Street.

The staff were placed in one of the outbuildings and the sick in another across the courtyard. Since everybody believed that being a doctor provided better protection than any other profession, there were name cards on all the doors saying: Dr. Wohl, Dr. Penson, Doctor, Doctor, Doctor... It didn't protect anybody from anything.

So we lived on the fourth floor in three rooms. There must have been about twenty people there, because every employee of the hospital was joined by his relatives, friends, and acquaintances who did not get "life tokens"[36] and were here illegally, thinking that this would protect them from the next roundup.

We all shared the same space. My mother and I had a tiny room that barely fit a bed. Pnina, who never left the house, cooked soup every day from real food substitutes. Sometimes there were even scraps of horsemeat floating in it.

Pnina lived with her husband and her boyfriend. It didn't even bother me. What did bother me was that no one objected when she would save for them the best morsels that swam in that thin soup.

My mother fell ill with typhoid fever. In almost every apartment someone had typhoid fever. By now, nobody paid any attention to the yellow notices about *Fleckfieber* stuck on the doors. Mama was very sick, but despite it, I slept with her in the same bed, and somehow, I did not become ill. Everybody said that I had a special connection with the lice.

When Mama could finally drag herself out of bed, she immediately went to work in the hospital. She only had to cross the courtyard.

When we heard the shouts in German, she was not at home.

The roundup had started.

Our apartment had a hideout. It was an alcove in the last room, behind an armoire. The armoire was wooden, with a double door, full of clothes; it completely covered the rather shallow alcove. In almost every apartment people made hideouts.

So, when we heard the German shouts, we all squeezed behind the armoire. There were a lot of us, I don't know how many, but we were so crammed in that you couldn't move an arm or a leg. It was hard to breathe.

The moment we moved the closet back in place behind us, the Germans smashed in the front door. We heard their voices and the banging of their rifle butts in the first room, then in the second room and in the kitchen. They were pounding the walls, the doors, moving something, overturning things.

---

36 Numerki życia, lit. life numbers. These were small cards supposedly exempting the bearer from transports to the death camps. Around 40,000 were issued to residents of the ghetto.

Sieh, a voice was shouting, *Sie mussen hier sein, es steht noch Kaffe auf dem Tisch.*[37]

They were getting closer. We froze even more.

Somebody's hand dug its nails into my arm. Another hand covered my mouth.

Now, they were evidently in our room. They were yelling something to each other. It seemed that there were two of them, but the blood was pounding in my ears and I couldn't hear a word. Now they were near the closet. We were petrified.

They opened the closet. They moved the hangers apart. They threw the clothes out. They hit the back wall of the closet. We were struck with terror. To this day I never experienced such terror.

Suddenly, we heard shots.

They left the closet and ran away. We heard their steps and the stamping of their boots. From the ground up, more and more boots were hitting the stairs, more and more German voices were calling out short commands. We stayed motionless. Our fear turned into a wrenching anxiety.

What could it be? Who did they shoot? My grandmother on the first floor? Marynka, who was sick and probably did not get away in time? My mother, who must have run from the hospital frenzied with her fear for me?

Yes, they must have shot my mother. I jerked forward. They held me back in an iron grip. I tried again. They hit me on the neck. There was nothing to be done. I was standing helpless inside an immobile and petrified human block. We waited. I don't know how long it lasted—maybe an hour, maybe three, maybe ten minutes. I don't know.

We carefully pushed away the armoire. The Germans were no longer there. Inside the room everything was overturned; things piled in the middle. Carefully, one after another, we stepped out from behind the armoire...

In the first room, Pnina's two husbands were sitting and cleaning their guns. They sat there calmly, as if there hadn't been any roundup,

---

37   German: "Look, they must have been here, there's coffee still on the table."

as if the Germans hadn't been here just a moment before. As if nothing had happened.

When the roundup started, they ran up onto the roof. They fired shots to lure the Germans out of the house, to save those people in the hideouts.

My First Encounter with Birth

The roundup was over. I snuck out and ran downstairs to look for my mother.

The doors to all the apartments were open. There was not a living soul anywhere.

The apartment on the third floor was empty. The table and chairs were toppled over, the burner of the stove left on, the kettle empty. Silence.

The apartment on the second floor looked the same. Here lived a doctor with a big family and my Warsaw grandmother. She'd somehow managed to hang on and live.

I entered carefully. In the first room there was dead silence, a wide-open window, and a blanket over the window. In the middle of the second room, there was a pile of clothes and books. Walking on tiptoes, I entered the third room. I froze. On a bed next to the wall lay my grandmother. On the wall above the bed there were splattered pieces of bone with snatches of hair, yellow stains, and a lot of blood.

Grandma lived in the first room. She must have been running away from them. She didn't let them take her alive.

In the ground-floor apartment, there was silence. I stepped inside. The stove was burning in the kitchen. It was the kind with a pipe going up to the ceiling. A woman was sitting at the stove with her feet in the embers. Her feet were burning; I can smell the stench. The woman wasn't moving.

This woman was a violin player. Everybody said that she was as talented as Grażyna Bacewicz.[38] Now, she was sitting in an empty apartment; her feet, swollen by hunger, lay in the stove.

I slipped down to the courtyard. It was dead still and freezing cold. The patients' ward was empty. All the doors were broken and the windows wide open; there was not a living soul around. The beds were empty, a blanket hung on a railing, and a bed sheet lay where it was thrown on the floor. Water was frozen in a glass on the table.

Where was my mother?

I rushed to the first floor. It was the same scene. Suddenly I froze. There was somebody there. The Germans?

Deep inside the room, among the empty beds, a woman was giving birth. Without a word, without a moan. Black hair glued by sweat fell on her forehead.

Next to her bed, there was a girl in the pink dress of a nursing school student, my classmate from a higher level. Next to her stood a doctor. I knew him; he lived in our building. He was young and joyful. He whistled, and whenever we met, he always said, "How are you, colleague?"

I stopped, hesitant. They didn't notice me. A moment later, I heard a piercing squeal. A newborn boy was arched upside down in the doctor's large hands. He was red, covered in mucus. He screamed!

I saw everything as if in a sharpened light. I saw the questioning look the doctor gave to the mother.

I saw when with a barely discernable movement, she nodded.

I took a second look, this time directed at the nurse in the pink dress.

With a sudden movement she grabbed a pillow from the next bed and pressed it down on the newborn. His squealing now became barely audible.

The roundup was over. From far away one could still hear shots.

38   Grażyna Bacewicz Biernacka (1909–1969), Polish composer and violinist, born in Łódź. Bacewicz was the principal violinist of the Polish National Radio Symphony Orchestra from 1936 to 1938. She lived in Warsaw during the German occupation and continued to give secret underground concerts. She taught at the State Conservatoire of Music in Łódź after the war.

Surgical Nurse

Sister Bajdycz was a beautiful woman. Tall and stately, she was probably Ukrainian. Her high cheekbones, smooth black hair, thick dark eyebrows, and beauty mark above her upper lip made it impossible for her to go unnoticed.

Sister Bajdycz was our instructor when the school of nursing was still on Czyste Street, and although she was younger than Sister Principal, the broad black ribbon on her bonnet indicated her high rank. She was an assistant nurse in surgery, a so-called surgical nurse, and now in the ghetto she was training us.

Everybody knew that Sister Bajdycz had a special relationship with the reddish-gray-haired head of surgery, which only added to her prestige.

When the ghetto had become a shooting gallery for the bloodthirsty German policeman nicknamed Frankenstein,[39] the surgery was located at the corner of Leszno and Żelazna. The streets were then covered with blood. Frankenstein would come to the ghetto in the morning and shoot at anything that moved until sunset, at whatever pleased him—straight, across, up, and down.

Wounded people were brought to the hospital all day long. The big operating room and the small ambulatory were busy day and night.

We were sitting in the hall on little stools around Sister Bajdycz, rolling cotton balls and folding antiseptic gauze. The cotton balls were easy. You just rolled a small piece of cotton with your fingers until it made a fluffy ball with a little tail, and it was ready. The gauze required more attention. The pieces of gauze often shred when cut into small squares. You had to fold in each edge very carefully four times, so that not even the tiniest thread stuck out.

"A surgical nurse must be very precise!" Sister Bajdycz would tell us. "A thread in the wound can mean the death of a patient." As if there

---

39   Josef Blösche (1912–1969), German SS and SD member noted for his brutality and sadism during the final period of the Warsaw ghetto. He also participated in the operations of Einsatzgruppe B in Belarus in 1941. Blösche avoided punishment until 1967, when he was arrested by the East German Stasi and executed two years later.

was nothing more dangerous in the Warsaw ghetto in 1941 than a thread of gauze left in a wound!

We were placing folded pieces of gauze on the trays, where they obediently awaited sterilization. The cotton balls, however, light and fluffy, were constantly falling onto the floor. Each time we made a move to pick them up, Sister Bajdycz would say, "Wait until you've finished and pick them all up together. A surgical nurse must economize her movements."

At that moment a shot was fired near the hospital. The bullet hit the window, and glass shattered all over us. A gust of air scattered the cotton balls and knocked off the bonnet with the black stripe. The bonnet rolled across the floor.

Someone ran in, pulling the wounded through the corridor; blood spilled, splashing the walls and staining the white fluff of cotton balls.

Sister Bajdycz didn't move to pick up her bonnet. We continued to work in silence. "A surgical nurse must stay calm."

Many years later, during the war in Chad, I was teaching a group of black girls how to cut and fold into small pieces the sheets we had hastily rinsed in the river Chiari. The wounded were being brought in all the time and there were no cotton balls and no sterilization. Before my eyes, I had the image of Sister Bajdycz.

To this day I can't, I don't want to, I try not to think of how she might have looked when they took her from the hospital and pushed her into the cattle car.

Umschlagplatz

I was caught only once at the Umschlagplatz. Until then, like other girls from the nursing school, I was protected by my pretty pink uniform. But on that day, they fell short in their head count for the daily quota, and in such situations, nobody stood a chance.

The Umschlagplatz, as it was known, was at the very edge of the ghetto. The train tracks reached almost to the big three-story buildings that had formerly housed some school. Trains would leave in the morning and in the evening, yet both the buildings and the square were always filled to overflowing with a tangled mass of people who sometimes waited several days to be loaded. During those few days and nights, they would desperately seek out some kind of hiding place. This was an impossible task because the buildings were wide and spacious, with no hidden nooks, and their attics and basements were already packed with people who had been caught earlier. Everybody seemed to think that a cellar or an attic could save them from death.

Herded with whips and shots, people would run from one floor to another.

Finding Ukrainians on the first floor, the crowd would run to the second. There the Jewish policemen would be waiting. So, the crowd would run back downstairs. Shots would be fired and the path would be blocked for a moment by a few corpses, and then the crowd would immediately rush back upstairs. More shots would be fired, some would fall and get trampled, while the rest would go as far as the attic, only to be driven back down to the exit, onto the square, where there was no escape and where the open wagon cattle cars were waiting.

The Ukrainians shoved them in—in any way possible. Sometimes, they had problems sliding the heavy doors closed because the people who had been shoved in kept spilling out. This could even have saved some of them from being taken in the transport if they hadn't already been smashed by the heavy doors that held them inside.

This was the end. In this rush, this hunt, there was no more room for anything human. There was nothing but wild animal-like fear and maddened perdition. How else can one explain the frantic mothers who dropped their children but convulsively held on to their string-tied parcels?

And on rare occasions—or perhaps not so rare at all, since how can this even be measured—one could see someone who was not fleeing, someone who was clearly not trying to run away from the cattle cars but toward them.

I didn't remain long in this crowd. I don't really know how long it was. Suddenly, a pane fell with a crash from some window above me and the glass scattered around. I looked up and saw Inka, who was standing at the broken window, giving me some desperate signs. The window belonged to the "hospital" room where—the irony of it!—there were still sick children. My pink uniform allowed me to rush into the "hospital." I was saved. I didn't even have time to panic. All that followed I watched already from the outside.

It was then, from that window, that I saw Felka. She was wearing a pink uniform too. That very day, Felka was supposed to "jump" over the ghetto wall. A friend of her parents had paid off the right people and she was supposed to be at the wall at dusk. She was a light blond and friends were waiting for her on the Aryan side. She had a big chance. And then, on this very day, they caught her mother. Felka saw her being driven in a rickshaw through the empty ghetto. She followed the rickshaw. A policeman tried to push her away: "You are young," he yelled, "you have to live."

They got to the Umschlagplatz and she rushed straight to the wagons. She made it at the last moment. Just when they were closing the doors, she spotted her mother, squeezed under the arm of a Ukrainian guard, and pushed her way into an already overcrowded cattle car, even though the Ukrainian was hitting her with the butt of his rifle, because there really was no space left for her.

I was told that it happened the same way when they caught Broneczka, who was left with only her grandfather because everybody else—her parents, uncles, aunts, and cousins—were already gone. So, when they seized her and herded her with the crowd to the cattle car, her grandfather, for whom there was no more space, latched onto the sleeve of a Ukrainian in order to get inside. He wanted to force the girl out and take her place in the cattle car. He was no longer capable of rational thinking, which would have told him that it made no sense whatsoever because everybody had to die anyhow.

There was still another story that circulated among people, although no one had witnessed it personally. According to this, someone had refused to get into the cattle car and called on the others not to let themselves be pushed in. They all perished in front of the train car, standing there, as if they were facing death in battle, even though they were not fighting, because they didn't have any weapons at all, but were shot standing there, as if they had been. And even though none of those who related this story saw it happen, it was the truth. A quiet, important truth that now, years later, no one talks about anymore.

Fredzia

In memory of Fredzia Kielbik, a twelve-year-old nurse in the Warsaw ghetto

Fredzia Kielbik was in our youngest unit.

Her mother was a nurse, but she died early on from typhoid fever. Her father was a broken, sick, starving man. Our director personally changed Fredzia's date of birth so that she could become a student, although she wasn't even thirteen yet.

She was a strong, sturdy girl. She hadn't gone through puberty yet, so her movements were abrupt and boyish. She wore black flats and made great, sweeping strides, as if stepping over some puddles. She shared the one-sixteenth part of a loaf of bread that she received every morning (and this was the portion for the whole day) evenly with her father, so that she was left with only a one-thirty-second part. Fredzia, quite naturally, worshipped the director and suffered when the other girls called her "Cow."

When the hospitals were closed and all the sick moved to Stawki Street (from where the trains left), we continued to walk there every day from the ghetto to take our shifts. The huge rooms had rows of beds in them, one next to the other, with no spaces in between. The patients lay there—three or four to a bed on dirty mattresses stained with excrement—bony skeletons with bedsores on every piece of protruding skin. They lay in the dirty brownish liquid spilling from their inflamed rectums, and nobody tried to find out the causes of their diarrhea—who was suffering from typhoid fever and who just from hunger. One way or the other, they were all condemned.

So, when those sick were already at the Umschlagplatz, there were, of course, no more bed sheets and no more windowsills needing dusting. The mattresses were dirty and stained, the human skeletons un-clothed. The only things left, paradoxically—as often happened in the ghetto—were the comforters. Someone must have discovered them in a forgotten warehouse, thick and cozy, with red fabric on one side and blue on the other. The director, who invariably came several times a day to inspect the "hospital," demanded sternly that we cover the beds, alternating the colors of the comforters: red side up on one bed, blue on the next.

There were already not many students left by that time. Most had shared the fate of their patients and all the other inhabitants of the ghetto. The pink uniforms did not evade the sweeps. You could not escape from the crowd herded onto the trains, even if you had documents from the so-called hospital.

Fredzia was among those who still remained. There were so few students left that during the night shift only one was left to take care of all those dying patients, and there were a hundred, two hundred, maybe three hundred of them. It was difficult to say.

The director always came at six in the morning. She would walk through the ghetto during the time of intensified sweeps, when every head counted for the policemen who had to deliver seven Jews each to the Umschlagplatz every day. At six o'clock sharp, she would enter the ward and check to see if all the sick had already had their morning *toilettes*. This consisted of rubbing their bedsore-covered backs with vinegar, or whatever we had, and powdering them with talc, which by some miracle was still available.

Every night, Fredzia rubbed sixty, a hundred, two hundred backs, moving the beds to reach every patient, and I would then cover them with blankets, alternating red, blue, red, blue... She'd start at two or three in the morning. When the director would come at six, wearing her navy blue cape with its red lining and a stiffly starched bonnet with black band, one could forget for a moment that all around the most dramatic "resettlement" in history was taking place, that captured people were just then filling the cattle cars, that clusters of them were being chased to the Umschlagplatz, that mothers, maddened by horror, were dragging their suitcases, but dropping their infants.

When the next day-shift nurses came to work, they would find that many of the sick who had just been rubbed by Fedzia were now dead, slowly stiffening corpses. No one had noticed, neither Fredzia nor—not surprisingly—their neighbors in the same beds.

One day there were not enough people for the contingent to fill the train, and the Ukrainians broke into the hospital to take the sick.

Fredzia did not hide. She could have easily crawled under the row of beds; it was all happening in the blink of an eye. But she did not crawl, and this is how her life ended. At twelve, Fredzia Kielbik was already a real nurse, and she followed her last patients from the Umschlagplatz to the train, just like Janusz Korczak.

"Remaining at her post to the very end," one might say. Only nobody ever wrote a word about Fredzia.

To Be a Pediatrician in the Ghetto, My Mother

My mother was a pediatrician. In the ghetto, she worked relentlessly and stayed there as long as the last child in the "hospital" needed her.

She worked first on Śliska Street at the Bersohn and Bauman Hospital and later on Leszno. And then... then, for some strange reason, the Germans left a little space for a children's hospital at the Umschlagplatz. Of course, this was no hospital, but rather a place to die, but at least the children could die in beds—two, three, four of them in one, some on the floor. Almost all of them had diarrhea. They were breathing very fast and looked like dirty, shriveled-up wax dolls.

Among those children was a four- or five-year-old girl, the daughter of a nurse who worked with my mother in the Drop of Milk[40] organization, when there was still a drop of milk in the ghetto. The nurse, not a young woman, was totally alone. The only good thing

---

40   The Drop of Milk organization (Kropla Mleka), established by the Polish-Jewish writer and journalist Mojżesz Altberg (1851-?) and his wife Paulina (1856–1938), was the maternity section of the Jewish Charity Society and provided milk, clothing, and other assistance to nursing mothers.

that had ever happened to her in her life was this little girl, Renia or Reginka.

Now Renia or Reginka was lying on one of the dirty little beds on the top floor of the building at the Umschlagplatz, waiting with other children for the day and hour when they, too, would be taken to the trains. In this hellish trap, there was no way her mother could even be with her.

If this hospital had been a real one and Reginka had been properly treated, there would have been no reason for her to die. But at the Umschlagplatz the problem was very different: it wasn't certain that she would die in time. And if she didn't do so, she could still end up being thrown onto the train and killed at Treblinka.

She succeeded.

I learned about it after the roundup. When I came back from work to our flat, I found Reginka's mother there, kneeling in front of my mother and kissing her hands.

Now everybody knows it, so there is no need to explain that at that time, in the ghetto, morphine and cyanide were as precious as gold. Only a chosen few had access to it. A small ampoule in your pocket gave you a wonderful feeling of safety, an assurance, a possibility of escape at any moment. To give someone else your morphine meant to give up your own chance for a quiet death at the moment of your own choosing and to consciously choose the horror awaiting everybody else.

And this is what my mother did: she injected little Reginka with her own morphine.

The Heart of a Jewish Mother

My parents' friends had a villa in Grotniki near Łódź. We went there sometimes on Sundays with some other friends. I hated those Sundays. They always started the same way: "She's grown so much! Soon she'll outgrow her mother! (I was six.) Only, why are you so thin? Don't they feed you? Her eyes just keep getting bigger. She'll charm them all; oh, she'll charm them!" Then the adults would talk, play cards or the piano. I was bored to death. In the springtime it was better, because if the weather was good, I could play in the garden.

The hostess was a nice, gentle, tall, and quite fat blond. I don't remember the host. They had an only son, Oleś. He was the apple of their eyes; their whole world revolved around him.

Mama told me later that after Oleś got his high school diploma (he had straight fives, of course), he'd been drafted into the army. For his mother, the world fell to pieces. It was inconceivable that her pampered, treasured son could find himself in a vulgar barracks among shorn recruits, where she could no longer hover over his fate. On top of it, this was the time of brutal street anti-semitism and Oleś had very black hair and eyes. There was no doubt that he would become a victim of harassment by corporals and other soldiers.

Oleś's mother moved heaven and earth. She secured dozens of certificates proving that her son in no possible way was able to serve in the military.

One evening, when we were in the middle of eating dinner, Oleś's mother appeared at our house. In her hand she held a small box which she handed to my mother. In the box was an oval ring. The large center of the ring had layers of garnets. The garnets were the color of dark red wine and looked like a bunch of ripe grapes. They were shining, as if every stone were a small live spark.

"But, why?" asked my mother.

"From happiness," answered Oleś's mother. "This is the heart of a Jewish mother."

Oleś was released from military service. His mother was standing in front of us and there were tears of true joy in her eyes. I never saw such tears again.

A few years later, we met Oleś in the Warsaw ghetto. The war had interrupted his legal studies and he was working as a clerk in the Judenrat.[41] He was alone. His parents had perished in the Łódź ghetto

---

41 German: Jewish Council. The Judenräte were German-appointed bodies responsible for administering Jewish affairs and liaising with the German authorities in German occupied parts of Europe. The first Judenrat was established in Poland in September 1939. Adam Czerniaków (1880–1942) was appointed head of the War-

at the very beginning. This way, he already had behind him what was still awaiting so many others. You could even dare say that, under the circumstances, he was quite privileged.

Sometime later, news blew through the ghetto that employees of the Judenrat would receive special passes protecting them from deportations. From time to time, such unconfirmed information would sweep through the ghetto like a wind, passed from mouth to mouth, and everybody immediately believed it. Unsurprisingly, it brought hope.

The information about protection for the families of employees caused an immediate wave of weddings. Every man who worked at the Judenrat could become a guarantee of survival. In a matter of hours, young and old women found life partners. Teenage girls were provided with instantly produced documents proclaiming new birth dates that made them adults.

No wonder that mama quickly arranged my marriage to Oleś. To me, Oleś looked like an elderly gentleman, especially because he was already starting to go bald. I don't remember how it all happened. All I remember is that he smiled at me, patted me on the head, and… disappeared. I didn't pay much attention.

A few days later, he was found hanging in the attic of the building that housed the Judenrat.

Mama never parted with the ring. She always wore it. It's amazing, but she managed to save it in the ghetto and during the Warsaw Uprising. When people asked about her beautiful ring, she would smile gently and answer, "This is the heart of a Jewish mother."

The war ended and we went back to our house with its little garden. Mama took great care of it. Whenever she had time, she would work in the garden. One day, she showed me proudly what a big patch she'd weeded and how her hands looked after this work. I looked—the ring was missing from her finger!

We dug through the whole garden, inch by inch, to no avail.

The heart of a Jewish mother had vanished into the ground.

---

saw ghetto Judenrat on October 4, 1939 and remained its head until his suicide on July 23, 1942.

The Cape

In elementary school, which in those days was called public school, I had a classmate named Klara. Klara was an exceptionally ugly girl. She was probably the ugliest child I've ever seen. She had a long face, eyes of an indefinite color, bulging like those of a fish, and a big, protruding nose that looked broken in half. Her nose stuck out of her thin face and attracted attention. On top of it, she had a very funny name—Studniporek. We never played with her during recess, of course, but not because of her ugliness or her funny name, but because Klara was different from the rest of us. She always walked with a book in her hand. Every day, during a break, she would take out a book from the school library, and she would read it after school while walking on the street.

One day, the librarian called Klara's mother and told her that she would no longer lend Klara books to take home because she was afraid that while reading them on the street, Klara would fall under a car. And then, who would be held responsible for it?

But it didn't help, because Klara joined a public library next to her house, though it was strange that they accepted a girl of ten. So, all that changed was that Klara now read the books on her way to school as well.

Sometime later, the librarian from the public library called Klara's mother and said that Klara had already read all the books for elementary schoolchildren and all the books for young adults, and she had now chosen a book by Proust that was definitely not appropriate for her. I don't know how we learned about it, but it did nothing to inspire our respect for Klara Studniporek. During recess, she still sat alone in the corner with her big nose hidden in the pages of a book.

Klara's mother was a small, poorly dressed woman who had a tiny grocery store near our school and who probably never read anything in her life other than the *Primer* from which she'd been taught to read.

Then the war started and I lost track of Klara as well as of the other girls from our class.

One day, already in the Warsaw ghetto, we were walking back from the hospital on Leszno to the dorm of the school of nursing. Suddenly, against the wall of some building, I noticed Klara. I had no doubt it was her, because nobody in the world had such a nose. She was horribly thin, so her nose seemed twice as big. She was squatting by the wall, squeezing a book in her arms. She was hugging the book, looking at it expressionless. I stopped, and the girls kept going. I noticed that Klara was shivering from cold. I covered her with my warm student cape from the school, thinking I had to bring her, right away, at least some hot water, since there was no longer any food at the school. I ran as fast as I could. The girl on duty gave me some hot water and I rushed back. Klara was lying on the dirty cobblestones. The cape was gone. Someone had taken it.

I bent over her. Her stiff, thin arms were gripping the book. It was the *Iliad*. Klara was dead.

Sometimes I wonder if her death had been any better because of my warm cape.

First Escape from the Ghetto

When the big roundup was over, my mother sent me out of the ghetto. I don't even remember how it happened, but one morning, when it was still completely dark, I found myself among the men of a Jewish work unit led by a policeman to work on the Polish side. They had special passes but were still checked for a long time. If you bribed both the Jewish and the German policemen, it sometimes worked, and you could leave the ghetto this way. On the Aryan side, you had to skillfully detach yourself from the group and, avoiding the *szmalcowniks*, disappear into the Polish crowd. Of course, all this was possible only if you had a place to go. And I had such a place. The people there were my parents' old neighbors and friends.

The professor had been with my father in the Radogoszcz camp and had been sent by the Germans to the General Government along with a group of other prisoners. He was hiding in Warsaw under a false name, working as a locksmith. He and his wife lived in a small room in the Wola[42] part of Warsaw. This was the address I had. I didn't know Warsaw at all, so I memorized a small map that they had drawn for me. I always got lost, but that time I got there easily. The front entrance was clear and I didn't meet anyone on the stairs either.

When I got inside, the first thing I noticed was the cream. On the windowsill stood a small glass of cream covered with a piece of paper. Next to it was a pot with a flower. The flower was blooming.

They were expecting me. A flowery tablecloth was on the kitchen table, with a plate on the tablecloth and white bread and butter on the plate.

I felt my throat choking.

I sat at the table. They asked me some questions. I didn't answer. I was still looking at this glass with cream on the windowsill and the spasm in my throat was getting stronger.

Was it because of little Abramek from the hospital on Śliska Street, who had never seen cream in his life and never would because he died just a day earlier? He was always calling me "Ala, Ala," and when I reprimanded him, saying my correct title was "Sister," he would smile and say, "Sorry, Ala, I was only joking."

I stayed there for three days. I wasn't allowed to go outside before they got me new documents. They were kind to me. For those entire three days I didn't speak. They understood.

On the third day, I ran away. The men from the Jewish work unit, possibly the same ones, didn't seem surprised. They made room to let me inside the group.

I went back to the ghetto. Running, I rushed to our fourth-floor apartment on Gęsia Street. My mother turned pale and burst out crying.

There really wasn't anything worse in the ghetto than to be a mother.

---

42   A major urban district in western Warsaw. It was the location of the greatest single massacre perpetrated by the Germans during the suppression of the Warsaw Uprising in August 1944.

Second Escape from the Ghetto

After the January roundup, I left the ghetto for the second time.

I'm ashamed to admit it, but I don't even know how my brave mother managed to arrange everything.

Later, I realized that I was nothing like Felka, who didn't "jump" over the wall but went with her mother to the train for Treblinka. I didn't stay with my mother in the ghetto. I didn't even argue against her decision.

Now, I think that in those days, one revealed one's real worthy forever. And I think that I am not worth that much.

So, I left the ghetto again, with an address on the Aryan side once more. This time, the people were not friends of my parents. The apartment belonged to a professor from Warsaw University. He was in a POW camp and there was no communication with him. His wife lived in this apartment on Wilcza Street[43] with, I think, three children. The apartment seemed big, with a long, dark corridor and several rooms.

The professor's wife opened the door and hugged me tight. Right away I was enveloped by her warm embrace. I instantly burst out crying and she cried along with me. She had the gentlest face I have ever seen in my life and the kindest, most tender smile.

I stayed there for some time. In the meantime, she got me false papers, including the real identity card of a deceased Polish girl called Alicja Zacharczyk. So, I could even remain Ala. Then she found me a place to live. And she vouched for me, saying that she knew my father, a doctor who was now in a POW camp with her husband, and from whom, as well, no letters came.

I moved to the Ursynów[44] part of Warsaw, not really giving much thought to the fact that the professor's wife had saved my life.

---

[43] A street in Warsaw's city center (Śródmieście) district.

[44] A southern suburb of Warsaw, south of Mokotów. At the time of the Warsaw ghetto it comprised mostly a collection of small villages along with some official buildings and estates.

Did God give it a thought when her older daughter was being killed in the Warsaw Uprising?

After the war my mother asked the professor's wife, "How will I ever repay you?"

The professor's wife just smiled her gentle smile.

Everything went back to normal. The war ended and the professor came back from the POW camp and started teaching at Łódź University. I was a student there, and like all my classmates, I shivered in terror before his exams. Fear, like everything in life, is relative.

The memory of that long corridor at Wilcza, where my steps had passed only a few years earlier, had now dimmed.

Bronek, the youngest son of the professor's wife, graduated cum laude in chemistry and had just started working when the attempt to blow up Lenin's monument in Poronin was made.[45] The organizers were discovered, and the police carried out searches all over Łódź. At Bronek's place, they found a typewriter whose keys matched the typing on some subversive leaflets.

There was a trial. He got out of prison as a marked person, forbidden to work in his profession. Time passed and the black hole of hopelessness deepened over the years.

And then a friend of mine came for a visit from New York—a biochemist and a professor at a medical school.

As often happens in very difficult times, against any logic and rules, he somehow managed to extract Bronek and bring him to America, where Bronek became a renowned chemist. He brought his wife from Poland and had a successful career.

One day, the professor's wife came to visit me.

"Thank you," she said.

Leaving, she stopped at the door and added pensively, "A life for a life?"

---

45   This refers to an attempt undertaken in 1970 by the anti-Communist underground organization Ruch to blow up Lenin's statue in the village of Poronin, located south of Kraków in southern Poland. The attempt was to coincide with the 100th anniversary of Lenin's birth. Communist police, however, arrested most of the plotters the day before the scheduled action.

9. The Jewish Nursing School students, Warsaw Ghetto, 1941.
Alina is not on the photo.

10. Alina during the war

11. Alina, Marek Edelman and Bund members, 1946–47

12. Alina and Marek in Nicea, 1950

13. Ala and Marek on vacation, 1950

14. Dr. Anna Margolis, Alina's mother, post-war photo

15. Alina with children with diabetes, 1959

16. Alina in the hospital named after Janusz Korczak

On the Aryan Side

The Zezaks

The professor's wife placed me with a family of architects in Ursynów. I've used the plural form here because both spouses were architects. Mr. Zezak might have been the chief architect or one of the chief architects of the city of Warsaw before the war.

He was handsome, with a small mustache and the inevitable pipe. She was tall—a bit taller than him—thin and slightly stooped. She moved in a fast, energetic manner. Her hair was greying—more gray than dark. Her most conspicuous feature was her left eye, which sometimes wandered to the side. It didn't happen all the time, but it still looked like a squint. That's why I called her Zezakowa—the Squinter. And that name stuck. Later, when my friend Zosia moved in with me, we called the whole family the Squinters—in Polish, the Zezaks.

They were good, honest, and courageous people, and great patriots. They had only one fault—they really couldn't stand Jews.

However, I was now called Alicja Zacharczyk and I was the daughter of a Polish officer deported to a POW camp. I had no mother. Taking care of me was, in a sense, a patriotic duty. The Zezaks fulfilled this duty very conscientiously.

They treated me like their own daughter. Mr. Zezak called me tenderly Aluetka. I had my own room in the basement next to the big kitchen. I took my meals at the table with all of them and participated in all big events like a rightful member of the family. We also celebrated my name day. Luckily, it turned out that there is a name day for Alicja in the calendar.

Mr. Zezak's two sisters also lived in the house. Both were spinsters. One of them, Aunt Aniela, was the epitome of goodness, and she showered me with such affection that sometimes I had an uncontrollable urge to tell her everything. Until this day, I'm not sure that she hadn't guessed it all on her own, but knowing the feelings of the family, she kept silent.

The Zezaks had two daughters. One of them, Jaga, was my age and instantly befriended me. The other, Grazyna, was a few years younger. Jaga was very cute, with wavy chestnut hair, a small nose, and a radiant, contagious smile. Grazyna was thin like her mother and similarly lacking in charm.

The Zezaks' home was a location for underground meetings. As a result of decisions made during those meetings, all three of us on some nights, would carry flowers and small white and red flags to decorate the graves of Polish soldiers at the cemeteries or the sites of street executions. I sometimes wondered what Inka, assigned to be my guardian by the organization helping Jews in hiding, would have said about it. At our every meeting, she kept telling me over and over again, "Be careful!"

In our garden there was a hidden stash of arms. We were not supposed to know about it, but we discovered a small window in the basement through which we could watch the moving shadows of young men who would pull out or put into the earth some barely visible objects during the night. Watching them, I felt as if I were in the very center of the underground struggle against the occupiers.

I was full of admiration for both Zezaks, who risked the lives of their daughters for the sake of the cause without any hesitation.

Twice, in a direct manner, I learned that the Zezaks couldn't stand Jews.

Our house was part of a little villa with two identical halves. In the other half lived the wife of a Polish general with her little son and a housekeeper. Her husband was in some camp and no letters came from him either.

One day, I noticed the housekeeper sliding under the porch with a bowl of noodles. I was very surprised because they did not raise any animals. When it happened again the next day, I crept under the porch from our side of the house. The maid didn't see me. Under the porch, huddled in a dark corner, sat two little boys. When I got used to the dark, I noticed that they were swarthy and one of them had a hat pulled down deep over his ears, with side locks visible from under the hat.

I wanted to tell Inka about them, but I didn't make it in time.

The next day, Mr. Zezak discovered the housekeeper's secret. He told her to get the children out. They were small and very dirty. They hung their heads. I couldn't see their eyes.

Mr. Zezak went to see the general's wife. I heard him yelling that he would not let her endanger his children and me, the orphan entrusted to his care. And did she even think about her little son?

I don't know what the general's wife said or if she even knew.

Helpless, in despair, I watched the children leave with Mr. Zezak, one on his left side, one on his right. He held them by the hands tightly.

They did not come back.

The second time was when the ghetto was burning. The glare was clearly visible in the sky. Jaga said,

"Do you see how it burns?"

And Mr. Zezak replied,

"What a pity Tuwimes[46] is not there."

This really was the Zezaks' only defect.

---

[46] A reference to the Polish-Jewish writer and satirist Julian Tuwim (1894–1953), his name distorted. Tuwim was a frequent target of anti-Semitic attacks during the interwar period with claims that his writing was alien to Polish art and culture, along with concomitant demands that his poetry be removed from school textbooks.

Easter, 1943, at the Ghetto Wall

It was a lovely spring day, April 19, 1943.[47] The sun was shining, a light breeze was blowing, and the gardens smelled of wet greenery.

Right after breakfast, I went to see Inka.

In the streetcar, people were saying that the Jews were shooting in the ghetto and that shots had been heard since dawn. And they were also saying that the Germans had shot a Polish boy scout on Niepodległości Avenue[48] during the night, so everyone should go there and lay flowers.

Inka wasn't at home. I ran to the ghetto wall. I got to Bonifraterska Street.[49] On Krasiński Square,[50] there were a lot of people, all dressed in their holiday best, already in spring fashion. There were little girls with jump ropes and balls. One of them was holding two colorful balloons. She was so pretty that everybody was smiling at her. The music played.

On the other side of the wall there was silence.

"Is it true that the Jews are shooting?" I asked some woman.

"Yah, true."

"The kikes are fighting. The Germans went in there," added a man.

And then I noticed that the Germans were guarding the wall. Every twenty, thirty meters there was a machine gun. Next to some of them, instead of Germans, were Polish policemen.

Shots were fired, both individually and in salvos.

I froze. My heart was pounding, my temples thudding. I bent over and patted the hair of the girl with the balloons.

There were more shots and some explosions.

---

47 April 19, 1943, was the starting date of the Jewish Ghetto Uprising.
48 A major north-south road running the center of Warsaw. The first street execution of Polish hostages (1943–1944) took place at 16 Niepodległości on October 16, 1943. The avenue ran through the Warsaw Ghetto.
49 A major street in the Nowe Miasto (New City) district of central Warsaw. Bonifraterska ran along the northern boundary of the Warsaw Ghetto.
50 A major urban square in central Warsaw. The square served as a buffer zone between the Warsaw Ghetto and the rest of the city.

My loved ones—mama, my brother, Inka—were on this side, but the others—our friends from the apartment on the fourth floor at 6 Gęsia Street, my classmates from the school, people from my building, my street, those in the shelters, those with guns and rifles...

The wall was not higher than a meter.

Almost across from where I stood, some youngster took a run up, as if pole vaulting, jumped over the wall, and ran into the ghetto.

Why? Who was he? What made him do it?

Nobody noticed, the Germans included.

There were more salvos. More shooting.

At around four pm, everything went quiet.

I had to go back. At home, there was an air of serene spring-time Easter.

The next day, I went back to the wall, back to Bonifraterska Street.

In the windows of a building across the street, on the ghetto side, I noticed two people. I thought I saw rifles. Someone was running on the roof.

Passersby and onlookers stopped in small groups and, raising their heads, pointed out to one another those on the other side. What they were saying about them I will not repeat. I don't want to repeat it.

In the afternoon, a huge fire burst in the ghetto. It could be seen from everywhere. Houses were burning; thick black smoke gushed up. The whole ghetto was on fire.

In the evening, in the sky above the ghetto, a huge, blazing glow appeared. The Germans were burning them!!!

For the next two days and nights, the glow got bigger. During the day, black smoke continued to pour.

When I went there again, maybe a week later, everything was still burning. The firemen arrived on Świętojerska Street.[51] They were try-

---

[51] A street running through Warsaw's central Nowe Miasto district. Part of the street was included in the Warsaw Ghetto. The brushmakers' shop, one of the main manufacturing enterprises in the ghetto, was located on Świętojerska Street along with several resistance bunkers.

ing to extinguish the fire behind the wall with water hoses, fearing that it would spread to the houses on the Polish side.

Gawkers gathered to watch from a distance.

I will not repeat what they were saying. I don't want to repeat it.

At the bottom of the wall, there was a hole, some kind of opening. A young girl was crawling like a snake towards us through this hole.

Everybody began staring at her.

She got out. She was all black, covered in soot. She was screaming so loudly that I could hear her,

"I jumped out! Everybody is burned!"

I heard a fireman shout back something like,

"Good luck, young lady!"

A moment later, a policeman pushed through the crowd, grabbed her by the neck, and pulled her with him.

The ghetto continued to burn for a long time, but there was no more shooting.

It was exactly there, at the wall, that for the first time in my life I felt really Jewish. And I felt that now and forever, until death, I would remain with those who'd been burned alive, with those who'd been asphyxiated and gassed in shelters, with those who'd fought and perished with those whose fate I hadn't shared.

What happened later?

Later, life followed its own course.

Mrs. Stefania

Today, few people know who Mrs. Stefania Sempołowska[52] was. "Miss Stefania," as she was called for a long time, lived to fight against

---

[52] Stefania Sempołowska (1869–1944), Polish educator, activist, and writer. Sempołowska is most noted as a prisoners' rights activist and supporter of equal education rights. She was a member of the Democratic Education Society and a co-editor of the youth magazine *Z bliska i z daleka* (From near and far).

human misery. She was always like that, and her friends called her "Stefania to the Rescue," after the title of one of her books.[53]

So, it's not surprising that during the war, her apartment on Mokotowska Street was a cauldron of crisscrossing causes, all focused on rescuing people. It was with Miss Stefania that my mother had found shelter after her escape from the ghetto. I didn't know about that. I was not allowed to know where my mother was.

Mrs. Stefania was already old and sick, never leaving her bed.

That night, while the glow of firelight rose over the struggling ghetto, someone was having a great, happy, and noisy party in her building.

Mrs. Stefania, bedridden for months, managed to drag herself out of bed.

"Shut the party down!" she screamed, "People are burning!"

The music stopped, and a deep, dead silence followed.

My First Encounter with Sex

Inka and Marysia were very young, maybe twenty-three or twenty-four, but for us they were great authorities. They gave us some sense of security, the feeling that, in case of need, we had somebody to ask for help.

Inka and Marysia took care of Jews who were hiding in Warsaw. They found apartments to which they brought Jews who'd escaped from the ghetto, distributed money received from London and made monthly payments to the owners of the apartments which were hiding Jews. They had to be very prompt and never late with the payments in order to protect people from being thrown out onto the streets. If an apartment was "hot," they had to find another one and move the endangered people, sometimes having only a few hours.

---

53 *Na ratunek* (To the rescue). The book recounts the rescue of the survivors of the Italian airship *Italia* which crashed in the Arctic in May 1928. Noted polar explorer Roald Amundsen disappeared during the rescue effort.

Many lives depended on their efficiency. For such young girls, it was tremendously responsible work. The room where they lived was kept secret, but anyway, they spent most of their time out of it.

That day, I came to see Inka in the afternoon. I absolutely needed to talk to her, but she was not at home. For a long time, I waited at the door, then I went downstairs not to draw attention, then went back upstairs again. Time passed; it was getting dark. Inka returned just before the curfew. She got very angry when she spotted me in the hall. There was no other way. I had to stay the night. We went to bed.

After maybe an hour or two, there was a sharp knock on the door. In one movement, I slid under the bed. Inka gathered some papers from the table and hid them behind a radiator. Again, the knocks, this time even louder. It seemed to me as if time had stopped, but an eternity might have passed as well. I tried not to breathe. My throat was dry.

I heard the door open. And there stood Zenon. He looked drunk; he was humming.

Zenon was a legendary character. Before the war, he had been a leader of the Jewish commandos who defended Jews from being harassed and demonstrated that they, too, knew how to fight. Now he was working in the underground. He was called the "Old Man," but I think that he was no older than forty-five, and he seemed ancient only to us. Zenon had a heavy beard and was rather thickset, with a strong build. He spoke loudly and in bad Polish. He behaved as if he wasn't a Jew hiding in occupied Warsaw. When he wanted something done, it had to be done instantly.

I was still very stupid, really infantile. I had never given much thought to matters of sex. I had never seen love scenes in the movies. I believed what the Zezaks' daughters told me, that Jewish women's sex was placed "crosswise." So, surprised that Inka did not signal for me to come out from under the bed, I continued to lie there motionless.

What was happening on the bed fell on me like the bombardment of Warsaw. I sank into a state of dumbstruck hysteria. I couldn't scream. I couldn't move. The bed was sagging, grinding, moaning. It seemed as if, in a moment, it would fall, then it was rising up again. I heard a scream and thought the Germans had come in. I was scared. It lasted forever.

When, shrunken and covered with dust, I woke up, the sun was shining and the room was empty.

This was my first encounter with sex.

Renia or Zosia

I knew Zosia from the ghetto. She was a nurse's assistant at the children's hospital on Śliska Street. No one knew that she was only fifteen, and anyway, back then it didn't matter. Zosia was then still called Renia Feldman, and everybody called her RF after a brand of injection needles. Renia was very pretty. She had short dark hair and blue-green eyes that were not quite symmetrical; one was a bit narrower than the other. It gave her face a slightly intriguing look. If not for the expression in those eyes, which was terribly sad, one could never guess that she was Jewish. She was developed for her age and very popular with the young doctors.

Renia, however, had her great love in the ghetto. She was in love with and was loved in return by a young surgeon. A year before the war, while working as a doctor at a summer camp, he met Renia, still a girl, who was a camper there. Their love had lasted a long time. Renia grew up. She was becoming a young woman. Now, with both of them in the ghetto, they were almost inseparable.

Generally, back then in the ghetto, love was blooming. Young people, old people, boys, girls, still children—all had usually already lost their families and were trying to find in love a bit of support, an escape from the everyday nightmarish terror. Their age didn't matter. One could see couples with a huge age difference. It didn't shock anybody. What mattered was to be together.

One day we were all standing at the hospital window, looking down at Śliska Street. In the middle of it, people who had been dragged from their homes were now walking to the Umschlagplatz.

The Germans hurried them, pushing them with their rifles. Suddenly, Renia screamed. At the end of the column were her parents and her little sister, Helenka. I knew Helenka. She was a sad, eight-year-old child, the apple of her elderly parents' eyes. Her mother was holding her hand tightly. Passing by the hospital, Helenka stopped for a moment and raised her head. A German hit her with his rifle butt. We froze. I squeezed Renia's arm with all my might. Nothing could be done. We knew that Renia would never see her parents and Helenka again.

From then on, she had only Henryk.

Sometime later, the Germans introduced the so-called "life tokens." At that time, people thought that having such a token was really going to save their lives. There were very few tokens. Their distribution was to be done by the Jews themselves. The tokens for the employees of the hospital were to be distributed by its director, Doctor Braude-Hellerowa. People forced her to do it because they trusted that she would not do anything vile, like giving tokens to her family members and friends. They were right.

One day, everybody was standing in the small courtyard waiting to see whom the director would confer with a "life token" and who would go to the Umschlagplatz. That was last time I saw Renia in the ghetto. She was standing on her tiptoes, hugging Henryk, her arms around his neck, and he was patting her head.

The next time I met Renia was on the Aryan side, when I was selling caramel toffee called "kaimaks." At first, I did not recognize her. She was as thin as before, very pale, but there was something different about her face. It had no expression, no emotion. We did not fall into each other's arms. Pretending was already my second nature.

Renia, or already Zosia, had jumped over the ghetto wall, and no one, absolutely no one, noticed. She just walked straight ahead. She had the address of some friends who owned an antique store before the war, as did her parents. She stayed there for three days. She didn't know what to do with herself next. When we met, she was heading for the wall, to get back to the ghetto or to let the Germans shoot her. As quickly as possible.

I took Zosia to the Zezaks. I told them that her father, who was a surgeon in Łódź, had been killed at the beginning of the war and that her mother had been deported to Germany for forced labor. Zosia had come alone to her aunt in Warsaw, I told them, but it turned out that the aunt had moved without leaving her new address.

As I said before, the Zezaks were exceptionally decent people and great patriots. They could not allow the daughter of a Polish officer to wander alone in Warsaw.

Zosia stayed with me. We lived together in my little room in the annex next to the kitchen and we slept in one bed.

My life had changed. I was no longer alone; I had somebody who really knew me. As if I had shrugged off some suffocating incubus, I suddenly became—we both became—normal, silly young girls. It was as if something had changed, although nothing had changed.

One day, Mr. Zezak's younger brother came to visit. They hadn't seen each other since the war had started, so it was a big family event. There was a festive dinner, with a white tablecloth and red-currant wine. Of course, the guest became very interested in our story and started to ask about the details of our life before the war, before we came to Warsaw. I managed quite well. My story was simple and did not raise any doubts. Zosia, however, as was often the case with her, gave free rein to her imagination. She said that her brother was a pilot, now in England. Unfortunately, it turned out that the new uncle was also a pilot. He asked Zosia:

"Has your brother already been *wylaszowany?*[54]

I shrunk. Zosia hesitated. Any slight mistake could bring disastrous consequences. Suddenly, I found a way. I simply asked,

"Excuse me, sir, but what does *wylaszowany* mean?"

We were saved.

Another time, in the evening, just before curfew, Inka brought Dawid. He had no place to spend the night. Our place was practically risk-free. No other family members ever came to our little room in

---

54   "Wylaszować" is a specialized term meaning making the first independent flight on a given type of aircraft.

the annex. Inka was supposed to pick him up before dawn. Dawid looked like "five Jews": He had curly black hair and a black beard, and his Polish was terrible.

Also, he was very loud, as if there was no need to be careful.

We closed the room and went upstairs for dinner. For some strange reason, the whole thing put us in a silly, exuberant mood. So, Zosia said,

"Do you know, Jaga, that there is a Jew in our room?"

To which I, choking with uncontrollable laughter, added:

"A Jew with a big beard! And he kissed Zosia!"

Jaga looked at Zosia, who was the object of her adolescent worship, and declared with all seriousness:

"Zosia, if it were true, then I...I....I would kill myself!"

Everybody burst out laughing.

Mrs. Zezak turned to me,

"Alinko, you were careless with washing the dessert spoons again."

Kaimaks

My duties included helping Mrs. Zezak with the housekeeping and the preparation of the caramel toffees called kaimaks. These kaimaks were basically the main source of income for the whole family. They were made from milk and sugar. The milk had to be slowly boiled with sugar in a big copper bowl and mixed constantly for three to four hours until it thickened and changed its color to a light brown. This required a lot of attention. The milk could get burned or spill over. In both cases, you had to start from scratch again and buy new milk and sugar, which meant big losses. When the milk with sugar reached the right consistency, the creamy mass was spread on big square waffles: a waffle, a layer of kaimak, a waffle, another layer of kaimak, until you had a "torte" covered with a shiny icing of kaimak. After the "torte" set, it was cut into small pieces, which were then sold to small and large stores. You had to enter the store with a big box of kaimaks, careful not to trip, and ask with an ingratiating smile,

"Would you like to buy some kaimaks?" I hated selling it. Every time I entered a store, I cringed with embarrassment. But not even once did it occur to me that while rambling like that around Warsaw, I might have been recognized as being Jewish.

One day, I was riding in a tram on Miodowa Street[55] with a huge box of kaimaks. The car was crowded. I was standing on the platform, next to the exit, holding the box outside, through the open door.

And suddenly, I noticed Henryk.

We had no idea what had happened to him. We didn't know if he'd stayed in the ghetto or had managed to get out. If he did get out, he had a chance—his "good" looks. He had light blond hair, blue eyes, and a square face with high cheekbones. He could pass for a peasant from a village near Warsaw. At night, Zosia and I spent hours thinking about what might have happened with Henryk. He was her only hope. She knew that besides him, she had no one left in the whole world.

And now, suddenly, I'd spotted Henryk from the tram. The tram was moving very fast, so I had no time to hesitate. I could not lose him. I jumped out, holding the box of kaimaks high above my head. They were saved (they always had an advantage over me), but I felt a sharp pain in my wrist. I bent over on the street, a small crowd gathering around me.

When I stood up, Henryk was gone.

It turned out that I had broken my hand. Every trip to the hospital was dangerous, but luckily, I knew where to look for Professor Tomaszewski,[56] a surgeon from Łódź, who had known me and knew about me. He had run away from a camp and was working in a shop as a locksmith. I went to see him; he immobilized my hand for quite a long time.

---

55   A street that runs through Warsaw's Stare Miasto (Old Town) district. The street connects to the Krasiński Square.

56   Wincenty Tomaszewicz (1876–1965), Polish surgeon. A graduate of Moscow university, Tomaszewicz subsequently took up work in various parts of the Russian Empire. He emigrated to Poland in 1922 and was appointed head of the Łódź Health Fund in 1925. Imprisoned at the Radogaszcz camp in November 1939, he was released in January 1940 and moved to Warsaw. In Warsaw, he worked under a false name at a hardware store. He led a team of surgeons at the Central Insurgent Surgical Hospital No. 1 during the Warsaw Uprising.

In time, the relationship between me and the kaimaks became openly negative: I hated the kaimaks and they were malicious toward me. If I left the copper bowl even for a moment, they would immediately spill over.

They were at their worst when I tried to read *Anne of Green Gables*.[57] I would run for a moment to my room and, before I could glimpse a few lines, the stream of brownish gluey mass was pouring through a gap under my door. Then, not only did I have to pour the new sugar and milk as fast as possible, before Mrs. Zezak discovered anything, but I also had to get on my knees and collect this hateful kaimak mass that crept into all possible cracks. As if in spite, the floor in my room was made of long planks and gaps. As if on purpose—a gap, a plank, a gap, a plank, a gap, a plank. The sugar and milk had to be replaced so that Mrs. Zezak would not notice. It took almost all my financial resources.

The business was best before the holidays. Then the "kaimak tortes," spread on big sheets of paper, took all the space in the house. The sale of kaimaks determined what would appear on our holiday table. So it was a great responsibility. The whole family was busy with kaimaks.

And then, a few days before Christmas, Marysia came. She stepped into the kitchen, where the kaimaks now took up two tables and the whole floor. She put her right foot on the kaimak near the stove and her left foot on the one spread between two chairs. The kaimaks were still wet, and the icing smudged on her heavy hiking boots. She slipped, and to avoid falling down, she supported herself by putting her hand on a third kaimak setting on a chair. Before we even had time to yell, it was over.

Before Christmas, all three of us were selling the kaimaks: Mrs. Zezak, Zosia, and I. Of course, each of us separately. The day before Christmas, out of the blue, Zosia announced that she would no longer sell kaimaks because she simply had had enough of it all. Now I know, of course, that it was not about kaimaks at all, but back then

---

57 Children's novel written in 1908 by Canadian author Lucy Maud Montgomery about a fictional orphan growing up in late 19th century Canada.

I was stupid, so I started to argue with her. Our fight lasted for a while. In the end, Zosia burst out crying and shouted through her tears:

"All right, I'll go, but I'll kill myself."

She grabbed a box of kaimaks and ran off.

It got dark. She still wasn't back. I went to the bathroom to brush my teeth. On the shelf there, I saw a few empty tubes of sleeping pills.

I somehow managed to get in touch with Inka, who took care of us. She came in a rickshaw exactly at the moment when Zosia, weepy and half-asleep, appeared on the doorstep. Inka took her to the hospital. More than anything, we were afraid that waking up in the hospital, Zosia would tell who she was.

She didn't tell.

The "Gorals"

On one particular day, we sold the kaimaks faster than usual, so we went to visit Inka and Marysia. It was a stupid and dangerous idea because theirs was a clandestine apartment and no one was supposed to go there except in an emergency. Very often, we did unnecessarily stupid and dangerous things, like, for example, riding the tram in the first car that was *Nur für Deutsche*.[58]

Only Marysia was at home. Of course, she gave us a piece of her mind. But, it turned out that we could actually be useful because "someone" was supposed to bring "something," and she was in a hurry to leave. So she left us alone. We had some tea and ate all the cookies. We felt happy and carefree. Then this "someone" came and brought the "something," and, suddenly, it got very late. We realized that we should have been back home half an hour ago. Rushing out, we grabbed a thick book that lay on the windowsill. Inka and Marysia always had great books, and we were happy to find something we could read for a whole week. We ran to the tram. This time, we took the second car.

---

58 German: "For Germans only."

It was terribly crowded. People were hanging on the steps, and the crowding inside was such that I thought my ribs would break. And still, at every stop, more and more passengers were coming. Suddenly, I heard Zosia's hissing whisper:

"Get down! Fast!"

For a moment, I thought she'd lost consciousness, that she'd suffocated and her brain lacked oxygen. Then I noticed that she was sliding down below people's shoulders and chests until she disappeared completely, leaving a empty space in her place.

And again the hissing,

"Get down!"

I stretched my neck to take up less space with my head, folded my arms, pulled in my stomach, and started to slide between the pressed human bodies. I heard cursing and swearing above, but below... on the floor of the tram... single and in piles... were brand new, blue-grey banknotes of 500 złotys, known in Warsaw as "gorals," because of the picture of a highlander (in Polish, a "goral") on one side. Again the hissing whisper,

"Get them! Fast! Stuff them in your blouse, and let's get out!"

It was not an easy feat. Collecting the money scattered between people's feet was almost impossible in this terrible crush. I somehow resurfaced and started to elbow my way forward, my movements hindered because I was squeezing banknotes under my armpits, in my pockets, inside my blouse, and in my folded arms.

It's hard to describe the comments of the public. "Snotty brat" was the most elegant phrase. I was inundated with the rich, colorful, and juicy vocabulary of the Warsaw street. Not paying it any attention, I pushed forward with my body, since my hands were occupied.

I performed a miracle. The tram was coming to a stop, and I'd already reached the front platform. People on the steps moved to the side, those in front of me got out—still holding fast to the railing in case the tram moved—and the wave of passengers poured out. I was outside too. But what about Zosia? In a moment, I saw her getting out with the next wave.

We were safe.

"To the entryway!" she yelled.

I have to admit that she always had better presence of mind. We ran into the first doorway, rushed up the staircase, and sat on the top-floor stairs. The house seemed empty and totally silent. We started to toss the money out of our clothes. It made quite a pile. We counted: five thousand, ten thousand, twenty thousand, and more, and more, and more!

Forty-nine thousand five hundred złotys!!!

We held a heated council. The tram was long gone and it was impossible to find out if anybody was looking for this money. And anyway, whose could it be? Such money must have been lost by some rich guy, maybe even a *szmalcownik*. But maybe by someone from the underground? In any case, there was no way to give it back. If it were a rich man, there was no reason to worry. If someone from the underground, well, we couldn't go to the police anyway.

We went back home. We counted the money once more, and then again. Forty-nine thousand five hundred.

That night we couldn't sleep. It was an enormous amount. What shall we do with it?

First, we will rent a room in Miedzeszyn[59] and leave the Zezaks. Then we will buy presents.

A beautiful radio for Inka and Marysia...

A watch for Celek....

The most expensive American cigarettes for Marek...

A thick warm sweater for Dawid....

Woolen gloves for Aunt Aniela....

We still had a lot of money left. So, day in and day out, we made new plans, changed our minds. We couldn't think about anything else.

About a week later, we snuck out to see Inka and Marysia to tell them about our good fortune. They were both at home. We had barely entered when they started to ask. Had we, by any chance, seen any money in their flat? They had left fifty thousand złotys in a book on

---

59   A neighborhood in Warsaw's Wawer district located on the eastern bank of the Vistula River, south of Praga.

the windowsill. The money was gone. They couldn't pay for the rooms where people in their care were hiding. They were in despair.

So, in the end, all that was lost was one "goral"—five hundred złotys.

The Cat

The year was 1944. Easter was coming. The sale of kaimaks went exceptionally well, which meant that we could prepare our first real holiday meal. For two whole days, Mrs. Zezak cooked from dawn to dusk. She covered all the finished dishes with white paper and placed them on the shelves in the pantry. On the Saturday before Easter, the shelves were full. Pig trotters in aspic were cooling in bowls; white chicken breast and white Polish sausages were arranged on the serving plates. A real crumb cake. And of course, Easter tarts—mazureks.[60] Beautiful mazureks glistening with chocolate icing.

I was excited. For almost four years, I had not seen such wonderful things up close. I was also proud because I'd had my part in it—kaimaks!

The pantry was in the basement, next to my room. Late in the evening, leaving the kitchen, Mrs. Zezak said,

"Don't forget to close the little window in the pantry before you go to bed."

I got up very early in the morning, when everybody was still asleep. I wanted to take another look at the prepared holiday breakfast. Alone, without witnesses. I wanted to look, to admire, to memorize.

The little window was wide open. White papers were thrown on the floor. Empty serving plates with leftover food were on the shelves. Pieces of chicken on the floor, smashed aspic, bitten-off cake, and mazureks!! On the remnants of the chocolate icing, I could see the clear

---

60   A mazurek is a traditional Polish pastry served during Easter. It usually consists of butter-sponge cake interspersed with marmalade with a layer of icing on top.

imprints of a cat's paws. Five claws and a dent, five claws and a dent. Like in the snow.

Across from the pantry, on a low wall, sat a cat. He was sitting there and quietly licking his mouth. I could see clearly that his paws were still smeared with chocolate. He was finishing his breakfast.

I had not closed the little window.

I can't even describe what went on later.

All I knew was that I hated the cat. I hated the cat with all my heart, which kept pounding like crazy, as if the Germans were pulling me from the hideout behind the armoire. My throat was constricted by this hate.

I hated the cat!

When I was escaping the ghetto, mama gave me a small ampule with cyanide: white powder that looked like confectionery sugar. Mama said, "Guard this like your own eye. Always keep it on you in case the Germans catch you. If they start torturing you and you can't stand it, if they push you toward a cattle car, don't be afraid. Break the ampule and swallow the powder. You will no longer be afraid and you will know nothing. So, don't be afraid. And guard this like your eye."

That's what mama said.

I decided to kill the cat.

Late in the evening, when I was alone, I poured some milk into a small bowl, broke the ampule, and poured in the white powder. I put the bowl on the windowsill.

I woke up at dawn and rushed to the pantry. The bowl was empty!

Across, on a low wall, sat the cat, carefully licking his paws, finishing his morning toilette.

The Ring

For a long time now, Zosia had harbored the idea in her head that we should go see the house where she used to live with her parents before going to the ghetto. Of course, this was another very stupid and very dangerous idea, and of course, we went.

Zosia used to live in a tenement building on Świętokrzyska Street. The building was as ugly as all the others around it. You entered it through a door that was shut at night with a bolt. On the lefthand side was a staircase, and, at the far end, an annex with a deep, narrow courtyard, enclosed like a well. Zosia's old apartment was on the third floor, and her father's small antique store was at the front of the building. Zosia's family had been in the antiques business for generations. They had lots of beautiful objects in their store.

For Christmas, Zosia gave me the only thing that she'd managed to preserve—a small gold ring with an oblong plate in the center, encrusted with three small garnets and three seed pearls. Giving it to me she said that the way to recognize a really old ring was to look for the solid gold backing under the stones. This ring had exactly such backing and was altogether simply gorgeous. An absolute marvel. I've never parted with it, not even when washing my hands.

So, one day, we went to that house on Świętokrzyska Street. It was noon; the street was almost empty. There was nobody at the entrance gate. Where the antiques shop used to be, they were now selling coal. Zosia grabbed my hand and I noticed that she looked like she was ready to cry. There were a few children in the courtyard playing hopscotch. One girl was skipping rope. We climbed up the wooden staircase as if entering a church—on our tiptoes, all solemn. Still not a soul around. We got to the third floor. We leaned on a wall across from the apartment door and stayed very quiet for a while, as if we were saying a silent prayer for Zosia's parents and her little sister, Helenka.

Then, Zosia gently stroked the door and we ran fast to the gate, happy that we'd made it.

The gate was closed and there was a huge lock hanging on the bolt.

We looked around. The children were still playing in the courtyard. Zosia tried to open the gate, but the lock would not give. A sense of foreboding descended upon us. Zosia knew of another exit through a small gate in the courtyard, leading to the next building. It was also locked. My heart was pounding. Zosia was dreadfully pale. It was becoming more and more obvious that we'd been discovered. I felt like a rabbit in a trap. All we could do was wait passively. After some time, which seemed an eternity, the lock made a grating sound and the gate opened.

There on the street was the janitor of the building, flanked by two Polish policemen. The janitor, without a word, pointed at Zosia. He had recognized her.

"You're coming with us, young ladies."

And here we were, walking along Świętokrzyska and then some other streets, straight to the police station. No one was talking.

They locked us in a small room. Then they left. We didn't talk to each other, but we knew that we were not going to admit to anything. After another while that seemed like an eternity or two, they opened the door and led us to an officer.

"So, are you Jewish?" He gave us a sharp glance.

"No!" I said.

He carefully inspected our documents, looked through a magnifying glass, and held them against the light. We both had really good papers, authentic, borrowed from some dead girls. He looked closely at Zosia who, on that particular day, really did not look Jewish, despite the fact that just a moment ago, on those stairs, her eyes had reflected two million years of the Jewish people.

"All right," he said, "We'll take a test." And looking at me, he commanded, "Pray."

I was sending blessings to my Nanny. I knew all the prayers and church songs. I began with "Our Father." He listened and then stopped me.

"And now you, young lady," he turned to Zosia. "Have you had your First Communion?"

"Yes," Zosia answered.

"Well, then, tell me how big is the wafer that the priest gives you at Communion?"

Zosia showed him her palm.

We were finished.

"And you are also Jewish," he added, looking at me, "only more clever."

They took us back to the small room. There, a young girl in a dirty kerchief was sweeping a floor full of cigarette butts. I took off the ring. Handing it to the girl, I asked:

"Will you deliver a message?"

She nodded. I gave her the address of the municipal office where Mr. Falski worked.

"Will you go? Right away?"

She looked at the shining ring, already in her hand, then slid it on her finger and ran out.

The time passed. We were sitting on a wooden bench on the edge of which someone had carved a heart and an arrow. We didn't say a word to each other. I was afraid. I was so afraid that I was feeling faint. I was thinking about mama, about the cyanide, and about the cat that hadn't died. I was thinking about what the Zezaks would say when they learned about it. I was afraid that they would find out. I was thinking about father telling me to be good to my brother, who was now in some orphanage and whom I would never see again. I was thinking about what Inka would say. Why had we done it? I was scared, scared, scared. I wasn't even thinking about the girl with the ring. We were lost. The time passed. It was getting dark. Nobody came. Why weren't they coming? Let them finally come. Suddenly, the door opened. There was a policeman in the door, a different one. He was older, fat, and fierce-looking. He beckoned to us with his finger to come to the door. I was shaking so badly that I could barely take a step. Zosia's head was bowed. In the room we entered were the two policemen who'd brought us there.

"Well, let's go little Jewish girls," they said, laughing. They took us to the street corner.

"And now, run back home."

The girl in the dirty kerchief had found Mr. Falski.

Mr. Falski got there in time and paid ten thousand złotys for us.

We were running to the tram when the girl caught up with us. She was panting. In her outstretched hand, she held the ring.

She handed it to me and ran away.

The Palm of a Hand

It was always Mrs. Halina, the seamstress, who went to Piotrków.[61] This time I was supposed to go with her because she had been seen there too many times and it was getting dangerous. It was supposed to be her last time. Then I would go there alone.

There was a camp for Jews in Piotrków, where they had been working in some factory, and those Jews at the Piotrków camp were preparing an uprising.[62] They were well organized. They already had the contacts to buy guns. All they needed was money.

Mrs. Halina had sewn the money into two belts, one for me and one for herself. They were invisible under our thick jackets. She also prepared a bundle with kielbasa for each of us. The train to Piotrków was crowded because it was a food-smuggling route. Bundles with kielbasa, lard, and chopped meat were stuffed under the benches. There was no hope of sitting, and I was squeezed, with others, into a half-open toilet. There were so many people that it was hard to breathe. At every station, new passengers arrived, with nobody getting off.

Suddenly, the train stopped in the middle of a field. A roundup? People ran to the exit, leaving their bundles. I felt a wild, sharp pain in my right hand. The pressing crowd had shut the toilet door on my finger. Everything went black. I felt I was going to faint, but then, what would happen with the money? Someone noticed and freed my finger.

Nothing special happened at the station in Piotrków. I followed Mrs. Halina from a safe distance, on the opposite side of the street. We entered a building and got to an apartment where some people were

---

61   A town located roughly 150 km southwest of Warsaw, in the historical Sieradz land (Ziemia sieradzka). Its name was changed to Piotrków Trybunalski after the Second World War and is presently part of Łódź province.

62   Piotrków was the site of the first official ghetto in German-occupied Poland, having been established on October 8, 1939. The majority of the ghetto remained in existence until October 1942, when it was "liquidated." A smaller ghetto consisting of around 3000 Jewish workers continued in existence until August 1943. A further 1600 Jewish workers were confined to two small camps outside of Piotrków until the winter of 1944/45.

waiting for us. We ripped open the belts, wrapped the banknotes in kielbasa, and put them into used sugar bags.

You could see the camp from the window, on the other side of the square. Twice a day the Jews would cross the square—at dawn, on their way to work, and at dusk, on their way back. Some had backpacks or bags. A few young Wehrmacht soldiers went in front of them and followed behind them. The sides of the column were not guarded. Nobody paid attention; everybody was used to it.

We were to approach them on their way back and pass them the sugar bags. Mrs. Halina was supposed to wait on the righthand side and give a parcel to the first man in the third row from the front of the column, and I—from the lefthand side—to the first woman in the third row from the end.

All was quiet; nobody paid us any attention. The woman immediately put the parcel I gave her into her bag. The column entered the camp, followed by the soldiers.

It all went surprisingly easily. I was supposed to meet Mrs. Halina at the station. The train to Warsaw was leaving in half an hour.

Suddenly, two civilian men appeared on either side of me. *Szmalcowniks*? I knew what I was supposed to do. But they were not *szmalcowniks*. They took me by the arms and led me to the camp.

I sat there for a long time, alone in a small, dirty room. Maybe half an hour, maybe two hours. What mistake had I made to end up like this? At what moment had I given myself away? Mrs. Halina went there so many times. Clearly, I was the one at fault. I had been careless somehow with a movement, a facial expression. I wasn't thinking yet about what they were going to do with me, only that I had failed.

Then, a German officer entered and sat behind the table. He spoke Polish. I knew what I was supposed to say, I knew it by heart. I wasn't even afraid. I was to play a stupid idiot, and I really was a stupid idiot. Suddenly, I heard Mrs. Halina's voice from the room next door. So, they had her too. And, right away, fear. What would she say? Would she say it absolutely the way it was agreed? I heard a German yelling a lot, but I couldn't hear her replies.

My German walked out and left the door half-opened.

And then I was seized with sorrow. So, this was the end. And nobody would know. Not even mama, ever. I was alone, alone, alone, and I would be gone without a trace. My poor mother. She had done whatever she could to keep me alive. And now I would be gone without even a trace.

Suddenly, someone's head appeared in the doorway. Then a whisper.

"Go to the toilet."

The head disappeared. A moment later, the German came back.

"I need to go to the toilet," I said.

He called a soldier and barked something in German. We went.

The toilets were in a small barrack, separated from each other by walls that didn't reach the concrete floor—like at a railway station. There was a knock—the soldier propped his rifle against the door. I was glued to the dirty, smudged wall. Now, I was really very afraid. I was shivering from the cold. My hand, smashed on the train, was hurting more and more. And there was the constant thought—I was alone, alone, alone, completely alone, no one would know.

Suddenly, under the wall, just above the floor, the palm of a hand appeared. It moved in and waited.

My hurting, injured hand reached for this palm and I felt a long, strong, and warm embrace.

And then nothing.

They stood us against a wall. Two Germans stood across from us. Their rifles aimed right at us.

Again, one of them barked an order and they fired. An inch above our heads.

They—the people for whom we'd brought the money—had given the Germans all this money for our lives.

At three in the morning, a soldier walked us to the station. The train to Warsaw was leaving in half an hour.

The Complex Childhood of Agata-Maria

I met Agata on the street. She was standing there with a basket selling pancakes. They must have been good because people were buying them. She would give them one cake wrapped in a paper napkin and the rest in a bag. That day I was hungry, so I bought myself a pancake. When Agata handed it to me in a napkin, I looked into her eyes and I immediately knew. She looked at me and also knew right away.

We agreed to meet in a few days and we went to walk along the Vistula.

Agata lived on the outskirts of Warsaw with an old woman who made the pancakes that she was selling. Every day she would stand on the street until she sold all of them. Then she dragged herself home. Once, some boys mugged her and took all the money. She was afraid to go home, certain that the old hag would throw her out. She didn't even want to think about what she would do then. But the old hag didn't throw her out. Who then would sell the pancakes?

Before the war, as a little girl, she lived with her parents in a nice big apartment in Kraków. Her father was a well-known architect, her mother a lawyer. They both worked a lot and Agata barely saw them. Twice, mama took her for a trip. Once, when she was six, they went on a boat to Denmark. The sea was stormy and Agata was throwing up throughout the whole voyage. The other time they went by train to Hungary and there was more bad luck, because Agata contracted hepatitis and spoiled the whole trip for her mother. Of both those trips, she remembered only the little mermaid in Copenhagen and the signs in Viennese cafés that she couldn't understand: *Juden Eintritt verboten*.[63] From this last trip, they barely managed to get back on the last train from Budapest because the war had just started.

When they got back to Kraków, the town was being encircled by trenches. Agata's father went to join the army but soon returned. Right after that, the town was seized by the Germans. Her parents packed some belongings into a few suitcases and went to live with her

---

[63] German: "Jewish entry forbidden."

grandma in Warsaw. But soon after that, they all had to move into the ghetto because it turned out that they were Jews, which Agata had never known.

Agata's childhood continued in the ghetto, which wasn't the worst of it until the Germans deported her mother and her little sister, who was born in the meantime. Agata was left alone with her father.

There was a church in the ghetto for converted Jews. Agata's father took her there for services and taught her prayers and rituals. When she had learned everything, he left the ghetto with her through a breach in the wall, for which you had to pay a lot of money to a Jewish policeman. For some time, they hid with her grandma's neighbors on the Aryan side. Later, the father managed to obtain the birth certificate of a Polish child and told Agata that she was now to be called Maria. One day, he sewed some money into her jacket and left for the countryside with Agata and her doll, Frania (with whom Agata still slept despite being a big girl now). He took Agata to a village and left her with some people who were supposed to take care of her from then on. He parted with her on the doorstep and told her what he had said many times before,

"Remember, you are no longer Agata, and don't tell anyone that you've ever been her."

Then, without turning back, he walked along a dirt road towards the railroad station and soon disappeared. Agata never saw him again.

She stayed with those people for the whole winter, but then her father stopped sending money. So, sometime in the spring, when the snow was still on the fields, they decided to send Maria away. Before sending her away, they checked her jacket and took the hidden money. Then they bought her a ticket to Warsaw and put her on the train with her doll, Frania.

"Someone will take pity on you," they said.

She got off at the station in Warsaw. She was cold, didn't know what to do, and started to cry. At some point, a lady approached and took her to her place. It was a room with a kitchen near the station. The lady had heavy makeup and looked tired. She fed Agata and put her to bed. She kept her for a few days and was so kind that Agata told her everything. She couldn't stay there longer, however, because men were coming to the room and they kept staring at her, surprised.

The lady gave Agata a note with an address where she was supposed to go, wrote a letter, and told her to follow her father's words and never, absolutely never, tell anybody anything. And most importantly, to never, absolutely never, tell anybody what her real name was.

Agata didn't remember how she managed to find the people whose address the lady gave her. In any case, they greeted her quite happily because they had small children and they were both working and had been unable to find help for a long time. Their apartment was on the fifth floor in a tall, dirty building in the Praga part of Warsaw, on the other side of the Vistula. There were two little rooms and a kitchen. They washed in the kitchen sink. The kitchen also had a small toilet encased in wooden boards. They put a cot in there for Agata, which she folded during the day because otherwise one couldn't pass through the kitchen. She was supposed to help with the housekeeping, cleaning, washing, and taking out the garbage, but her main duty was to take care of the children. There were four of them: the eldest was five, the next one three, and the last were eighteen-month-old twins.

Agata would get up at five, when the children were still asleep, and prepare anything that needed to be done before they woke up. Then she would take care of the children until the evening, when the mother would return from work. If the weather was nice, she took them for a walk. The most difficult part was to get down from the fifth floor with the twins' carriage. She would do it floor by floor: first the carriage, then the children, and then again, until they got down. On the way back, she would leave the carriage in the entrance hall. In the beginning, she was so tired that she thought that if she'd lay on the ground, she would never get up. But with time she got used to it and thought only how lucky she was to have a place to sleep and not be thrown out onto the street.

One day, when she was walking with the children, it seemed to her that on the other side of the street she saw her father. She forgot everything else, left the children, and ran across the street among the honking cars. On the other side, she spotted him again, farther away, in a crowd. She ran for a while, not able to see him anymore, but still ran and lost him. Desperate, she understood that she would not find him. She wasn't even sure if it had been him.

Then she realized that she'd left the children alone. When she ran back to where she'd left them, she found some women and the janitor of the building standing around the carriage. They were yelling and cursing at her.

That evening she was told to pack her things (which all fit into a small bag) and get the hell out. It was already after curfew, so she spent the night at the entrance to the building and in the morning trudged onward. She wanted to get to the Vistula and jump off the bridge. And then—luckily, such things happened in those times— a small boy, younger than herself, with a stack of newspapers under his arm, appeared before her. He didn't ask any questions; he just said: "Come."

He took her to a church where there were a few other boys like him. It was a hideout for the newsboys, whom we might now call street kids. She stayed with them.

And then the newsboys found the old woman who was frying pancakes.

I made a date with Agata to see her in a week. I wanted to take her to Inka.

But a week later, on August 1, 1944, the Warsaw Uprising started, and, like so many others, I never saw Agata-Maria again.

To Jump from a Train, Bronek's Story

One evening, we finished washing the dishes after dinner and went straight to bed. We were tired. It was very dark. The bushes in the garden rustled, although there was no wind.

Suddenly, we heard something that sounded as if someone were scratching on our window. The basement window was small and covered with overgrown shrubbery.

We both sat up in our bed. There was nothing. And then, as before, this scratching, like a cat or a dog, barely there. And then again, nothing. Zosia whispered:

"Go."

I got out of bed and walked over to the entrance door, barefoot. They were still awake upstairs. I could hear Mr. Zezak's voice. I opened the door as quietly as I could. It didn't creak, as if conspiring with me. I looked out—there was nothing. But a moment later, I noticed a shadow glued to the wall behind the door. It was long and narrow. I waited and the shadow waited. Then I asked,

"What?"

He slid noiselessly inside. Now I knew for sure that he came for us. I put a finger on my lips, took his hand, and we walked downstairs. Upstairs, they were still talking quietly. They didn't notice.

Zosia was standing in the middle of the room, very tense.

We noticed that the shadow was shaking like jello. He was probably cold, but mostly he was very afraid.

The shadow turned out to be Boruch, or rather Bronek.

He stopped shaking and we fed him. He was fifteen, tall and thin, with light hair and a lot of freckles. He had a small nose, not at all Jewish. And clear blue eyes. He probably would have been long dead if not for his looks. We put him in our bed as the third occupant. He slept like a stone. The next day he spent under the bed to avoid being discovered in our room by Mrs. Zezak. Then, Inka found him a hideout in Wola.

He had been captured with a friend at the Umschlagplatz during the July action. They let themselves be pushed to a cattle car without any resistance because they had already planned what to do. They held hands tightly in order not to be separated. They had been together since the time of the first action, when they had lost everyone. Baruch had lost his father, mother, three sisters, and grandmother. Adam had lost his two older brothers and their wives. Until then, they had all lived in the same apartment, so when the Ukrainians rushed in there, the two of them simply hid under the table covered with a tablecloth with a long fringe—and stayed there. The Ukrainians simply didn't notice them.

Since then, they were inseparable. They slept wherever they could, often in empty staircases. They ate or not, stole from restaurants for the Gestapo, and ran from the police. They were joined by others: first Rysiek, then Abram, then Jurek, then Felek, Dawidek, and Szymek, and a few others. They grew into quite a gang. They were all fourteen or fifteen, with Rysiek, the oldest, at sixteen. They knew they couldn't let themselves be caught. They knew what was awaiting them if they were caught.

Once, when Abram was caught by a policeman, they jumped out of an entrance hall, threw themselves at the policeman, hit him, and bit him until he let Abram go, holding on to just a shirtsleeve.

This was when they decided to stick together and to jump out of the cattle car if they were caught. They had a heated discussion about how they would do it. Some thought that they should push the door open and let the whole crowd jump out. They calculated that if thirty people jumped, maybe ten could save themselves. Others said that they were not strong enough to push the door open, and they could not be sure if they could count on the grownups because they had families to take care of and would be afraid. Moreover, the grownups might not believe that they have to jump and that if you didn't jump this would be the end. So, they decided that it would be best to prepare saws, saws small enough to fit in their pockets, in order to saw open the window. In every cattle car there was a small barred window. If they managed to get to the window and started sawing, three of them together, the bars should give way. But then, they would have to squeeze through the window one by one, so they probably would not all be able to make it, because after two or three of them had jumped out, the Germans would start shooting. So this wasn't a good solution either because no one could be left behind. They still hadn't decided how they would do it right up to the very end, but they all had those saws in their pockets.

Of course, they did not manage to stay together until the very end. Every evening, when they snuck off at dusk like cats to their agreed place, they would see, in despair, that one or two were missing. These were black days. Jewish policemen were fighting for their own lives. They were told to bring seven people each to the Umschlag-platz, so they would bring seven.

When Abram didn't come, they thought that he'd found another hideout, but when Jurek and Szymek didn't come either, they all understood. So then, Boruch and Adam decided to hold hands all the time. Day and night.

And that's how they were caught. Holding hands made their escape more difficult. They were pushed into a cattle car. A German hit Boruch with a rifle butt. He staggered but didn't let go of Adam's hand. There was such a crush in the cattle car, it was hard to breathe. But they knew they had to move toward the window. Inch by inch, they elbowed through. They didn't know how long it took, but they finally got there. Pushing out the door was out of the question. What could just the two of them do? They didn't know how long it took them to get the saws out. Squeezed and pressed together, people couldn't move even a finger, not to mention a hand. And they had only one hand free, because they were holding each other tight with the other.

And then they started to saw. The stunned people didn't pay any attention to them. They didn't know how long it took, and they were almost half-conscious when, to their surprise, one of the bars gave way. Adam seemed to faint and Boruch continued sawing alone—or, rather, his saw kept moving by itself. And then another bar gave way. And then the rest. Then people noticed and started to jump. There was slightly more space around the window. Boruch pulled Adam out from under people's feet and pushed his head through the window. It went through. Boruch pushed, and Adam's shoulders and then the rest of him went through to the other side. Boruch wanted to put his head in the window, but someone tried to push him aside. So, he first had to fight off the other man. Finally, he succeeded. He was very thin and his bones were narrow; he pushed his shoulders sideways, and then his pelvis. He fell onto the embankment, and then someone jumped behind him. Then he heard the shots.

Long after the war, at some Warsaw party I chanced to attend, I heard two very famous and important people discussing various successful techniques of jumping from the cattle cars. And I remembered Boruch.

What would he say? Would he say anything at all? His method was invented by Adam and him together, but he never saw Adam again. Which means that the method was not successful because the point was never to jump out alone.

When Boruch woke up on the embankment, it was night. He staggered along a thick grove, and when it got lighter, he noticed some huts. He snuck into a dog house—the dog let him in; it didn't bark—and he slept there until dusk. When he awoke, the dog was licking his face. It soothed him. The dog's tongue was wet and gentle.

Luckily, he didn't meet any people.

He walked night after night, eating grass or carrots stolen from a field, and somehow, not quite knowing how, he approached a city. It was Warsaw.

He had no idea what to do. He didn't know the city. He only knew the ghetto.

But he knew one thing: he had to look for Adam. So he walked and walked until he came across some railroad tracks. These were the tracks he was looking for. He followed them for a long time, searching in the bushes, checking under branches, leafing through the trees. Looking for a trace. He couldn't recall if he ate anything or where he slept.

He didn't find Adam.

He got back to Warsaw. Luckily, he looked just like many local boys, so no one paid him any attention. Now he called himself Bronek. He stole rolls from the street stalls. Days passed, maybe weeks, and he couldn't see a way out. Not that he really cared.

And then he met Zoya. He met her just like that, when he was stealing apples from some basket. Zoya was selling those apples.

Zoya was the only girl in their gang. He hadn't thought about her, didn't know that she'd left the ghetto.

They sat down on a low wall and did not say a word.

But then she explained to him how to find our place. How did she know about us?

Inka found him a hideout in Wola, and we would go there from time to time to deliver money. There were eight people in the hideout: two women, one child, and five men, including Bronek. Everything seemed surprisingly quiet, so even their fear calmed down. Everyday life. And then hope. And then, unbelievably, the joy of life.

They left their hideout on the first day of the uprising. They ran straight through the Warsaw streets madly happy, passing boys with white and red armbands. They built a barricade alongside the others.

Only the women and the child stayed in the hideout.

Bronek, or rather Boruch, was killed by a stray bullet on the first day of the Warsaw Uprising.

The Decision, Szymon's Story

Just before the curfew, Inka brought us Szymon.

She tried as much as she could to avoid endangering us this way, but sometimes she was desperate because otherwise she would have to leave someone on the street. She threw us a curt, "Until tomorrow," and rushed out to get home on time.

Szymon was well-dressed and clean-shaven. His eyes and eyebrows were terribly black.

Before I even had time to say a word to him, I heard Mrs. Zezak's footsteps on the stairs. I shoved him into a narrow space between the closet and the window, where he could barely fit because he was quite big. At this very moment, Mrs. Zezak opened the door. She was laden with parcels, which she put on my table, and slumped down heavily upon a chair.

"I barely managed to buy the waffles for the kaimaks. I've got such a big order."

She had never done this before. She had never come downstairs to my room. Fear grabbed me by the throat. It always began with my throat.

She took out a notebook from her purse and started to write down her expenses—another thing she had never done in my presence before. The fear in my throat was growing.

I could hear the breathing from between the closet and the window.

"The order is for tomorrow. We have to start cooking kaimaks at six in the morning. I'll come and help you," she said.

She had never come down at six in the morning.

The breathing sounded now like the locomotive in Tuwim's poem for children. It was impossible for her not to hear it.

She got up. She went to the kitchen and walked around aimlessly.

She'd seen, she'd heard, she knew. She was now thinking what to do. She was giving me a chance.

"Good night."

And she went upstairs. Her heels clicked on the steps to the bedroom.

Szymon was pale as a ghost. His eyes seemed even blacker than before.

Szymon had come to Warsaw from Vilnius.

He rode—He walked—He rode—He walked.

Not from Vilnius itself, but from the Vilnius area. In other words, from the forest.

In Vilnius, they were armed and organized into fighting units. They decided to leave for the forest and to fight the Germans there. When Szymon's unit left the ghetto, there were about thirty of them, including four girls. They didn't know what had happened to the rest. When the Germans broke up their unit, there were only three of them left. They lost each other almost right away, and he was alone. He wanted to get to Warsaw where his sister was living in the ghetto, but when he got here, everything was already over, and the Warsaw ghetto was no more.

Szymon talked the whole night. He would stick his head out from under the bed and whisper. I hung my head down to hear him better. Our heads touched.

He would talk, then fall asleep, then wake up and talk again.

And I with him. I would listen, fall asleep, wake up, and listen again.

He was talking about Him. He was their commander. The commander of all the fighting units in the Vilnius ghetto. He was a communist, but they didn't care about politics, and it didn't matter. Thanks to Him, they were so well organized. Thanks to Him, they were armed. They decided that after they were armed, they would leave for the forest one by one. And they gradually left.

He was older than the rest of them, in his mid-thirties. He had a wife and two children. He could have hidden on the Aryan side, but he didn't want to leave the ghetto.

When the leaders of the underground were called to the office of the head of the Jewish administration, they didn't hesitate to go. They thought it meant negotiations of some sort, because by then they were a force to reckon with. Instead, they were told that the Germans wanted His head. The Jewish policemen seized Him and took Him to the ghetto gate, but the fighters got Him back. He went into hiding and they protected Him.

And then everybody was told that the Germans had given an ultimatum: If He didn't surrender, the entire ghetto would be liquidated at once. There were only twenty thousand people left. Seventy thousand had already been killed, mostly in Ponary.

They were told to meet and make a decision. Szymon would remember it all his life, every day and every night. They all gathered. First His party comrades and then all the leaders of the ghetto resistance had to decide: His life or the lives of the twenty thousand. One fighter or the twenty thousand lives of the condemned.

So, even though everybody knew that the fate of those thousands had already been decided and that their road inevitably led to whence no one ever returned, they didn't know how to decide.

They couldn't decide.

So, they decided that He had to decide. Himself.

Szymon repeated this one word again and again: decide, decide, decide.

And it was not about the decision itself, which was clear from the beginning, but that they had forced Him to sentence Himself to death.

They had betrayed Him, abandoned him.

They had left Him to face death alone.

They watched helplessly as He walked to the office of the Jewish head of the ghetto. They waited at the entrance, but they never saw Him again. They led Him out through another door to a waiting Gestapo car.

They were told that He had swallowed cyanide. Some said He had been tortured to death. Many different stories were told later, but this is not important.[64]

Soon after, they left for the forest. Szymon thought that there might have been hundred and fifty of them, maybe two hundred. But this isn't important either.

I don't know what happened to Szymon.

The Thirteenth House, Luba's Story

Luba came to us in the middle of the day. I had never met her before.

Entering, she bumped into Mrs. Zezak, who politely showed her the way and even accompanied her to the kitchen. She didn't suspect anything because Luba had a fabulous Aryan appearance. She had light, smooth hair, blue eyes, and a small, straight nose. Still, despite this, she was followed by the *szmalcowniks* all the time and constantly had to change apartments. Her stay at our place could become dangerous, but for the moment there was no other solution. We had to hide her. During the day we locked her in the closet, and at night she joined us in our big bed. Two days later, Marysia found her a place in Miedzylesie near Warsaw.

---

64 Szymon was likely recounting the story of Yitzhak Wittenberg (1907–1943), a member of the Communist party and one of the leaders of the Vilnius-based Fareynikte Partizaner Organizatsye (United partisan organization). Wittenberg was arrested by the Jewish police but quickly rescued by members of his organization. The head of the Judenrat, Jacob Gens (1903–1943), then demanded that Wittenberg surrender himself. Fearing a potential massacre of ghetto residents, Wittenberg surrendered and was later found dead in his prison cell having supposedly swallowed cyanide.

Luba's whole family remained in Janów. Her little brother, however, tried to run away and had been hung by the Germans on the porch of their house. Later, she learned that the rest of her family had also been murdered. But back then, she was pushed onto the train alone.

Just before Treblinka, someone tossed a few of the children out of the train car. Luba didn't even know how it happened. She just rolled down onto the ground. Then she got up and noticed the distant lights of houses. She didn't know that it was Treblinka. She didn't know anything. She just walked towards the houses. The night was dark. She said that she'd knocked on twelve doors. Six didn't open at all, she remembered. Two opened and were immediately shut again. In four houses they let her in, but when she asked for water and shelter for the night, they didn't give her any water and they shut the door fast, she remembered.

When she got to the thirteenth house and stood at the door, a family was sitting at the table: a father, a mother, a rather big boy, and four little girls.

The father said, "They come here every night searching for you, people. Look!" He made a broad gesture, pointing at his family, "You can see that I can't take you in."

And then the boy asked his father to let her stay and said that he would hide her so well that no one would find her. He hid her in the barn under the hay. At four in the morning, when it was still completely dark, he woke her up and showed her the road to Warsaw.

And she went.

The moment Luba got a Polish visa (and since she now lives in Israel, this happened forty years after she left), she went to Warsaw.

At the airport, she rented a car and went to the town of Treblinka. She went from house to house looking for that boy. They all remembered her and claimed that she'd spent that night with them. But she knew she hadn't. At the thirteenth house, a woman was doing laundry in a washtub. Nearby, a man was cutting wood.

She was already quite tired, so she asked for some tea. They sat at the table and she told the woman why she had come to Treblinka. The woman thought for a moment. She seemed to remember her late father-in-law telling a story about a little Jewish girl who'd gone all alone on the road to Warsaw.

"And where is his son now?" Luba asked.

"It's my husband, the one cutting wood."

He said he often wondered if she'd survived. Now, he couldn't believe that she really had, that she was standing there, with her hair dyed black, in front of him, a man already graying.

Since then, she comes to Poland every year. At the airport, she gets into a car and goes to Treblinka. The driver, always the same one, says that at some distance from the town, she gets out of the car and continues on foot.

Is she visiting the people who saved her or her little brother and parents who couldn't be saved?

The Uprising

My Patient

When the uprising broke out at 4pm on August 1, 1944, we were in the Okęcie[65] part of Warsaw. We were supposed to move the Jews who were hiding there from one hideout to another. Suddenly, there was a commotion in town. We noticed white and red armbands on many sleeves. We needed to rush back to Inka, who was in the Old Town.[66]

We made our way through the city, passing people running in different directions. In some places barricades were being raised. The white and red armbands were everywhere. It took your breath away.

We walked for several hours and finally got to Miodowa Street. In the house where Inka lived there was now a field hospital. Inka was a doctor and we found her there. Zosia left me and ran to look for Julek, with whom she'd fallen madly in love two weeks earlier.

Fighting had started in the Old Town.

---

65 The largest neighborhood in the Włochy district of southwest Warsaw.
66 Stare Miasto, a neighborhood in the central Śródmieście district of Warsaw and the oldest part of the city. Stare Miasto was leveled during the Warsaw Uprising and subsequent German military operations. The neighborhood was almost completely rebuilt following the war.

Soon, the wounded appeared in the hospital, including even one Wehrmacht soldier. They were lying on beds. The organization of the hospital, prepared by the underground, had not failed.

Several girls, both young and old, who wanted to work as nurses, gathered around Inka. Only two or three among them had been directed there by the underground structures of the Home Army.[67] Others—some of them still almost children—happened to be there just by chance. Inka accepted all of them, even twelve-year-olds. There were no doctors, so nurses not only had to care for the patients but also to dress their wounds. Inka walked among them, showing how it was done. As a student of the nursing school, I had a great advantage over all the others. Only now did I realize how important it was.

Hell started very quickly. The Old Town was under fire. Bombs were falling. One hit the house next door. There was a huge thud and everything was covered in a thick, gray-brown dust that swirled in the air, preventing you from seeing anything. It got into your throat and clogged your nose. I started to run away, senselessly. I rushed ahead over the piling rabble, unable to see anything—other people running around me. After some time, I came back to my senses and went back.

People were digging up those who'd gotten buried. The hospital was full.

It seems that you don't learn anything from experience, because years later, in San Salvador, I started to run away and senselessly rush ahead in exactly the same way when the first house crumbled during an earthquake.

The next bomb fell on Miodowa right after the first one. I thought it had hit the hospital. The wounded who couldn't move looked at us

---

67   *Armia Krajowa*—the main internal resistance force in German-occupied Poland. Organized in Febuary 1942, the Home Army was affiliated with the Polish government-in-exile and eventually numbered 390,000 members in 1944. Led by General Tadeusz Komorowski (1895–1966), the Home Army was the main Polish force during the Warsaw Uprising.

from their beds with helpless despair. As it turned out, the fate awaiting them was worse.

Fighting continued the next day across Miodowa, on Długa Street.[68] Shooting could be heard, followed by silence, then shooting again. Inka told us to run to Długa and check and see if there were any wounded, and if so, to bring them to the hospital. There were many wounded. They were lying at Długa on the pavement, on the street, in the recesses of doorways.

We scattered like sparrows, each of us to her own wounded patient. Mine turned out to be rather old and tall. He had wounds in his thigh and arm, and there was no way that he could get up, even with my help. He had to be dragged. He was very heavy. I was big and strong (in the ghetto they'd even called me "Sister Tower"), but I was still unable to move him.

I felt like crying. On top of everything, the shooting had started again. Bullets ricocheted from the cobblestones right next to us. Suddenly, I felt a sharp blow to my leg. But no, nothing had happened. What to do? I looked at him in desperation. He smiled at me weakly and tried to pat my head with his undamaged hand. He propped his good leg firmly against the street, I pulled with all my might and... success... I had moved him a step. This way, I slowly dragged him to the hospital. He was bleeding a lot and he fainted when we reached the door. But he had been already saved.

However, it turned out that some shrapnel did get me. In my pocket I had two small celluloid dolls that I'd taken from our home in Łódź and which I always carried with me. I considered them my good luck charms and was very attached to them. Now I took them out of my pocket, totally shattered. A bullet or piece of shrapnel had hit them instead of me and had probably been deflected.

They simply sacrificed themselves for me. It made me sad.

---

68   Located in the central Śródmieście district of Warsaw and one of the oldest streets of the city. Długa Street was the scene of heavy fighting during the Warsaw Uprising with its eastern section remaining in insurgent hands until September 2, 1944.

I took care of "my" wounded patient until the end. He turned out to be a very important commander. We became friends. I even told him the truth about myself—my real name and how I happened to be there. Later, when we were leaving the Old Town, I helped him slide into a sewer manhole. And it was not easy at all.

It was on the last day, and the Germans would be arriving at any moment. We had to hurry and the manhole was narrow. Only Home Army fighters, understandably, were let into the sewers. Panic had begun. A crowd of people who lived in the Old Town gathered around the entry. They were pushing, trying to shove away the fighters who had led the uprising. There were tears, shouts, curses, the law of the fist, and strong elbows.

The wounded on the stretchers couldn't be evacuated. The stretchers did not fit into the manhole. Even today I find it impossible to erase from my memory the image of those wounded. When the Germans came, they set fire to the hospital on Miodowa along with the wounded in their beds.

"My" wounded patient could already stand up, but his left leg was immobilized, so he was pretty wobbly on his feet. But if he hadn't been able to stand on his own, he wouldn't have had any chance at all. I supported him until the last moment. Fortunately, since he was a very important commander, the soldiers made space for him and let him in right away.

He disappeared into the sewer without a glance at me. It was understandable. I never met him again.

We got into the sewer because the insurgent mayor of the Old Town fell in love with Inka and gave an order to let us in. The dirty, fast, whirling water sometimes reached up to my nose (luckily, I was tall). It was impossible to see anything and you had to move in total darkness, touching the one ahead of you to keep the rhythm and direction. From time to time, we passed those on the side who'd run out of strength. Some were dead. Despite being completely intent on moving forward and not falling, I was still thinking about my wounded patient. I was sure that he wouldn't make it. It seemed impossible he could endure this hellish road on his one leg.

But he did make it.

Many years later, when I was already a physician, I received a notice to report and collect the Cross of Valor.

In my mind, I offered it to my celluloid dolls.

The Saved Leg

The fighting in Mokotów[69] was very brutal. Nothing like in the song from those days of the uprising, which proclaimed that "these August nights and our supple arms are all we need."

When the peasant passing by with his cart by a field of stubble found Barbara there, she was lying unconscious in a pool of blood, her leg almost severed. The peasant placed her on his cart and brought her—together with her barely attached leg—to the field hospital. The hospital was crowded, filled with wounded people lying all over the place.

The peasant, now also all covered in blood, carried Barbara in and tried to find a place to put her down. Since there was no place, he left her on the ground and went to look for help. The doctor came, gray with fatigue, and called to the nurse, "Prepare for amputation."

The nurse bent over Barbara and fainted. It was her sister.

"Let's wait with the amputation," she begged the doctor.

There was always a bunch of children sitting on the steps of the hospital. They were maybe eleven or twelve-year-old boys and girls who were used as messengers. The adults couldn't move around because the Germans were everywhere and would immediately start shooting. For some reason, they didn't pay attention to children.

The nurse, trembling, prepared small cards. She wrote a professor's name on each one, along with an appeal: "To the hospital—immediately!" The professor, an old and experienced surgeon, was their

---

69   The main southern district of Warsaw. Mokotów was heavily Germanized following the occupation with numerous Reichsdeutche and Volksdeutche settling in the district along with SS and German army barracks. It was the scene of heavy fighting during the Warsaw Uprising, leaving almost two-thirds of the district in ruins.

father. After he was miraculously released from a camp, he'd gone into hiding by working as a locksmith in a workshop in Warsaw. From there, he'd gone straight to operating on insurgents.

She told the children to go everywhere where there might be doctors and look for the professor. The children scattered. She looked after them for a moment. They ran hunched down, looking like little puppies. In a moment, they were gone. Barbara was pale as paper and getting paler. Her sister, the field nurse, sat next to her, helpless. The surgeon came back twice.

"You will be responsible if she dies," he said.

When he came a third time, she caught him by the sleeve.

"Let's amputate," she said.

At that moment, the professor stood in the doorway.

He operated on Barbara for hours in this field hospital. He saved her leg.

Later, I found the professor in a real hospital in Grodzisk.[70] Barbara was lying in a real hospital bed.

It would have been a pity about the leg.

Promyka Street

It was already after the uprising. The population of Warsaw had been marched to a camp in Pruszków.[71] From there, the majority of those capable of work were sent to Germany for forced labor. Those who remained behind tried to find shelter around Warsaw.

By some inexplicable miracle, I found my mother, about whose fate I hadn't known anything. Now, my brave mother was working as a nurse in the camp in Pruszków, always dressed in the outfit of

---

70   A small village on the northeastern outskirts of Warsaw. The village had a population of around 300 prior to the uprising.

71   Transit Camp 121 (*Durchgangslager 121*) was set up on August 6, 1944, to process civilians expelled from Warsaw during the uprising. It operated until mid-December 1944, during which time some 400,000 people passed through the camp on their way to forced labor or concentration camps.

a German *Schwester*, always wearing a cap on her head, hiding her black hair. She was busy trying to get people out of the camp to save them from deportation to Germany. She distributed money from London among the Jews in hiding. Here, in the camp, she was very well known. Many people came to her with their problems and somehow no one realized who she really was.

One day, we got information that a group of Jews, fighters from the Warsaw Uprising, remained in empty Żoliborz[72] after the exit of the civilian population. Now the Germans were searching the whole quarter and the people hiding there were in great danger.

These were our friends from the Jewish Combat Organization (ŻOB)[73] who had managed to get to the Aryan side after the fall of the ghetto. After the outbreak of the Warsaw Uprising, when it seemed they could emerge from hiding in the liberated part of Warsaw, they'd decided to form a unit in Żoliborz that later defended a position on Mostowa Street.[74] They joined the People's Army[75] because in some of the Home Army units the mood was antisemitic, and it was dangerous to reveal who you were. Marek tried to do so and was severely beaten in the Old Town. Then Julek tried, and he barely escaped with his life.

There were three members of the command of the Jewish Combat Organization in this group:

---

72 A district in north Warsaw located along the Vistula River. Żoliborz capitulated on September 30, 1944, during the Warsaw Uprising, and emerged from the fighting relatively unscathed.

73 The Jewish Combat Organization (*Żydowska Organizacja Bojowa*) was established on July 28, 1942, during a wave of deportations from the Warsaw Ghetto to Treblinka. The ŻOB, led by Mordechai Anielewicz (1919–1943), was the main resistance force during the Warsaw Ghetto Uprising, during which most of its members were killed. Survivors of the organization participated in the Warsaw Uprising.

74 A street in Warsaw's central Nowe Miasto district. The scene of heavy fighting during the Warsaw Uprising, all the buildings on the street were burned down or destroyed.

75 The People's Army (*Armia Ludowa*), established on January 1, 1944, was the partisan wing of the Polish Communist Party. The People's Army refused to join the structures of the Polish Home Army for ideological reasons.

Antek, or rather Icchak,[76] represented the ŻOB on the Aryan side. He was a tall, very handsome, dark-haired man with a light mustache and blue eyes who could have easily passed for a Pole, except for the fact that he did not speak a word of Polish.

Celina, or Cywia,[77] was the only woman in the command of the ŻOB. She was tiny, ugly, and unimpressive, with not a shred of feminine coquetry. She was very wise and had great authority.

Marek,[78] the deputy commander of the ŻOB (and the commander of the unit in the area of the so-called "brush makers") became the commander of the ŻOB after the death of Mordechai Anielewicz. Marek looked so Jewish that no one could make a mistake. He had black hair, black Jewish eyes, and was very thin, which made all those traits even more pronounced.

The others:

Zygmunt was a lawyer, a mature man, older than the others by some fifteen years. He was very tall. He didn't look like a Jew, mostly thanks to his light Polish eyes. As it turned out later, Zygmunt's height became a serious problem during the clandestine exit from Warsaw.

Tadek or Tuwie, a ŻOB fighter, was a small, quiet, and inconspicuous blond-haired man.

Julek was also blond, but his very Jewish nose betrayed him. It was Julek who embarked on a very dangerous adventure trying to join a Home Army unit. He was recognized as a Jew and it was only by a miracle that he survived. Julek was gentle and shy, with a very nice smile. He had met my friend, Zosia, just prior to the uprising and they'd been inseparable ever since.

Marysia, or Bronka, was a ŻOB liaison on the Aryan side. Physically, Marysia had a major asset—eyes that were blue like forget-me-

---

76 Probably Icchak "Antek" Cukierman (1915–1981), a deputy commander of the ŻOB during the Warsaw Ghetto Uprising. Cukierman was tasked with procuring weapons and ammunition on the Aryan side during the uprising.

77 Probably Cywia "Celina" Lubetkin (1914–1978), the highest-ranking female member of the ŻOB and one of its cofounders.

78 Marek Edelman (1919/22–2009), last surviving leader of the Warsaw Ghetto Uprising and subsequent husband of Alina Margolis.

nots, round like small plates, and full of pure innocence. Her looks saved her many times from serious danger.

Tosia, a doctor from the Bersohn and Bauman Hospital—small, frail, older than the others—was a very brave woman. Her husband, a non-Jew, was in a German POW camp.

And finally, there was my friend Zosia.

So, Marysia and Zosia heroically emerged from their hideout at Promyka Street[79] and all alone, without a compass or any sense of direction, walked through the razed and deserted city, where not a living soul was left. As happened in those days, they avoided capture by the Germans and reached the camp in Pruszków, and from there got to the Red Cross Hospital in Boernerowo.[80] The director of this hospital was Dr. Stanisław Świtoń.[81]

Doctor Świtoń did not waste a minute. He immediately organized a convoy of the Red Cross, which was to go to Żoliborz with stretchers under the pretext of evacuating two severely sick women. I don't know how I ended up in this convoy. I suspect that my mother organized it. Besides me, there were four other people: Barbara, two young men whom I didn't know, and Marysia, who knew Żoliborz and was supposed to guide us. As it turned out after the war, one young man and one girl were a couple and also Jews who, after the ghetto uprising, had hidden on the Aryan side. In this convoy, going to save some Jews, only one person was a non-Jew. Luckily, Doctor Świtoń didn't know about this, but, strangely enough, we didn't recognize each other either. It was fortunate.

---

79   A half-kilometer long street in Warsaw's northern Żoliborz district near the Vistula River with villas and allotment gardens.

80   Boernerowo, a neighborhood in the western part of Warsaw's Wola district.

81   Margolis is likely referring to Dr. Stanisław Śwital (1900–1982). Śwital worked as a sanitary doctor with the department of health of the Warsaw City Council. He was active in the underground and a member of the Polish Home Army. Along with Dr. Janusz Korczak he organized assistance for the Jews in the ghetto. He served at the headquarters of north city center district of the Warsaw section of the Home Army during the uprising. Following the defeat of the uprising, he ran a small hospital at Boernera 33 in Boernerowo.

We left in the morning and reached the outskirts of the city. There we were stopped at the German guard post. It was a small booth with two Germans in uniform. Barbara spoke German and told them our fake story. We also had a certificate stamped by the Red Cross. And the stretchers. They believed us and let us go. They told us to return before two o'clock.

We entered Warsaw. We walked through the ruined, empty city. We knew that the Germans had mined everything. This was the most dangerous part. Despite having survived the uprising, I was clueless about the mines. I thought that one had to walk very carefully, taking the lightest steps. I took off my shoes and walked barefoot. When it was all over, everybody laughed at me, but I didn't see anything funny about it.

The worst part was that we absolutely couldn't figure out where we were. Everywhere were the same ruins and not a trace of a street. Promyka Street lay on the bank of the Vistula, so we aimed towards the river. We walked for a very long time and there was nothing. We were in despair. One moment we thought we should go right, then left. Clearly, we were lost. There was not a living soul around. Just a desert of ruins. Time passed; it was almost noon. We started to worry. The Germans had allowed us to stay in the city until two o'clock. This was getting dangerous.

Suddenly, Marysia shouted:

"It's here!"

We were on Promyka Street. An orderly row of small, identical houses ran along the small street. They had not been destroyed. Each of them had a small garden. In the gardens, the shrubs were blooming. It seemed like a fairytale. The sun was high. It was afternoon. There was complete silence. Now, finding number 25 was not difficult.

The little house seemed abandoned. We entered the garden. The front door was open.

They were all in the basement. For the last two days, the Germans had been searching the neighborhood, and this very day, in the morning, they had already been in the basement of the neighboring house. Their voices and banging on the walls could be heard clearly. At noon, they always stopped working and went for lunch. They could come back at any moment. They usually came back at two. If we had come ten minutes earlier, it would have been all over. We would have walked straight into them. Now we had to act immediately, as fast as possible.

They left the basement, one by one, squinting in the bright light. We spread out the stretchers. On one of them we placed Zygmunt, who was sick and had no strength to walk; on the other we put Marek, who was not fit to be seen if we were stopped. Zygmunt's legs, since he was very tall, stuck out from under the blanket. And his shoes were an "insurgent's" shoes—half-calf, laced. We covered Marek's head to make him completely invisible.

We started back. Now it was easier because you just needed to know the general direction for leaving Warsaw. The stretchers were heavy, but we didn't feel the weight. We took turns carrying them.

I didn't know then that I was carrying out of Warsaw the future father of my children.

We walked back through the ruined city. At some point, around five in the afternoon, we noticed the outpost. Now fear set in. We were supposed to come back at two and it was already five. Five of us had enetered and now twelve were leaving. Even if we could account for the two on the stretchers, it still left ten. What could we say? That there were more people sick than we anticipated? And the men would attract attention. Besides, none of them had documents. The closer we got to the guards, the more the tension rose. The most at risk was Marek, with his unfortunate Jewish looks. He could bring suspicion on all the others.

We approached the post. Two Germans were smoking cigarettes; a third one was cleaning a rifle. We put the stretchers on the ground. Zygmunt's military boots were sticking out, hopelessly, from under the blanket. We got closer and... These were not the same Germans! The guards had changed at two o'clock, and these ones didn't know how many of us had entered. Despite the danger, joy gurgled in my throat. They checked the first two identity cards, mine and Barbara's, both of them authentic. Then one of them approached Marek's stretcher, reaching with his hand to lift the blanket. Approaching, he asked whom we were carrying. Dead silence. Julek was as pale as paper. I couldn't see anything anymore. I was waiting for a shot.

At this moment Barbara said in German,

"Achtung! Fleckfieber!"[82]

She said later that the words came out by themselves, unexpectedly, without a thought, as if a flash went through her and at the end of this flash was this *Fleckfieber*.

These words saved us. The Germans were terribly afraid of typhoid fever. The one who was approaching Marek's gurney and almost had his hand on the blanket jumped away as if burned and yelled,

"Alle raus! Schnell!"[83]

And with a fat index finger, he pointed in the right direction. We grabbed the stretchers and rushed forward.

A room with beds was already waiting in the hospital. They were all signed into the reception book as patients.

Doctor Świtoń died a few years ago. It's unbelievable but we never went to see him. One can think about that however one wants.

He was posthumously awarded the title "Righteous among the Nations" and a tree was planted for him in Jerusalem.

---

[82] German: "Watch out! Typhus!"
[83] German: "Everyone out! Quick!"

Epilogue

We all moved together to a hideout in Grodzisk. There, we were joined by Lodzia and Luba, who was then called Marysia. So we had two Marysias. This other Marysia, Luba, was as thin as a stick and very pale. We called her Green Marysia.

There were twelve of us in two rooms on the first floor of a little wooden house. The entrance to the second room was covered by a thick curtain, behind which the men would hide.

On the ground floor were the German headquarters for the fight against the "bandits." It was always full of soldiers, commanded by a fat major, whose booming voice made the whole house shudder. He didn't pay any attention when Marysia and I would leave to go shopping. He had his private quarters in the courtyard. There was a lamp, a radio, and a small bookshelf. The major spent a lot of time there. We could often hear him singing a gentle song: *Es geht alles vorüber, es geht alles vorbei... Nach jedem Dezember kommt immer ein Mai.*[84] I still remember it to this day and I like it very much.

---

[84] "Es geht alles vorüber, es geht alles vorbei" (Everything passes, there's an end to it all), a popular song recorded in 1942 by the German singer Lale Anderson (1905–1972).

One day, Soviet tanks rolled down the narrow street in Grodzisk. We all came downstairs. People stopped and watched in silence. I later read that the tanks were greeted with flowers. I didn't see it.

Then the war ended. I returned to Łódź, my city. I passed my high school exam. I went to medical school and became a pediatrician. I got married, had two children. Just like everybody else. But something seemed to drive me to those places where misery was the greatest, as if I were looking for this misery on different continents. So, was I really like everybody else?

My mother survived. When the war ended and the whole world went crazy with happiness, she learned that my father, for whom she was still waiting, believing that he'd come back, had been killed by the Germans in November, 1939, in a small forest near Łódź.[85] So, her life as a woman ended when she was forty-three.

My brother also survived. When mama sent him out of the ghetto, he ended up in an orphanage where nobody knew anything about him, and that's how he survived.

So, she saved both of us. My brave mother.

My father was forgotten by all. The world changed and people changed. I noticed this only many years later, because I had been, of course, busy with other things. All I could do for him was to place a plaque on the wall of the Jewish Cemetery in Warsaw, because the Jewish Cemetery in Warsaw is sometimes visited by people who come to pay their respects to those who were murdered. It is also visited by many foreign Jews. On this plaque, I described in a few lines his forgotten life.

My husband, Marek, became a very good doctor, but he was only interested in treating those patients who were expected to die. A few years later, a book was written about him, translated into other languages, and he became famous.

---

85   Aleksander Margolis was shot in December 1939 in the Lućmierz forest near Zgierz, north of Łódź, as part of the German *Intelligenzaktion* against members of the Polish intelligentsia.

There was never any news about my father's German friend, Hans Werner.

The Zezaks.... Mama and I went to see them just after the war ended. We found their address with difficulty. They lived on the fourth floor of a poor, dilapidated building in Praga. Their house in Ursynów no longer existed; it was destroyed by a bomb. Mama wanted to thank them because, after all, it was thanks to them that I was alive. We rang the bell, Mr. Zezak opened the door, looked at me, looked at my mother, and slammed the door shut.

Inka, my guardian on the Aryan side, got married for a short time, had two daughters, and worked in Poland as a pediatrician. She wrote a memoir that robs you of your sleep. She died of cancer.

My inseparable friend, Zosia, left with her husband and son for Germany. We see each other every few years.

And the others?

When we left Grodzisk, just after those Soviet tanks rolled into town, our paths separated. Some of us stayed in Poland, others left.

And, seemingly, everything goes on as it goes on for everybody else.

But, are we, we from those times, like everybody else?

17. Alina, 1985

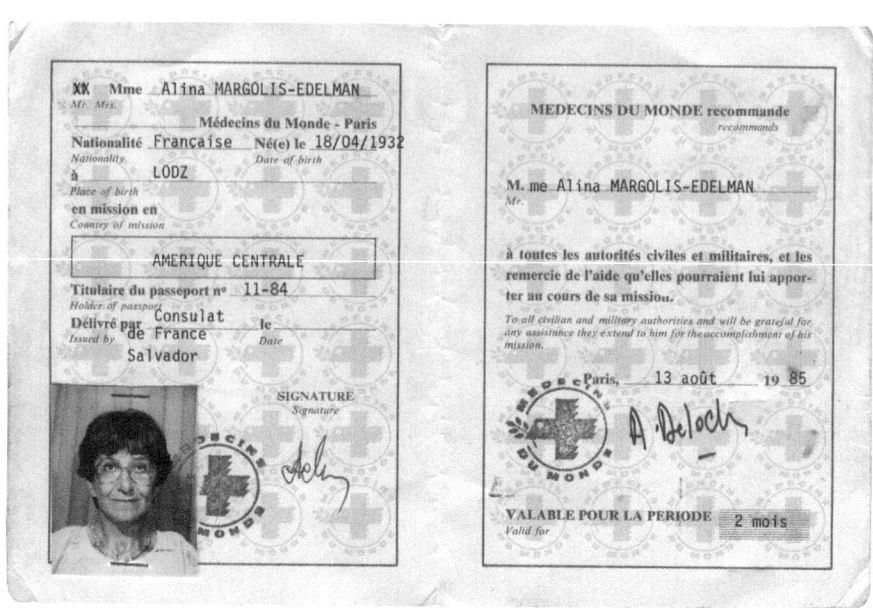

18. Alina's passport for her work in Salvador, 1985.
She changed her birthdate by ten years.

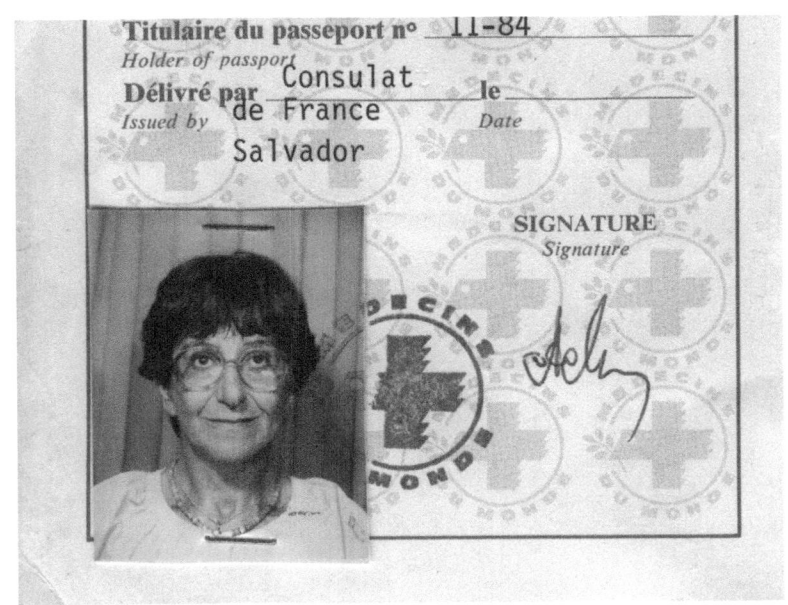

Titulaire du passeport n° 11-84
Holder of passport
Délivré par Consulat le
Issued by de France Date
Salvador

SIGNATURE
Signature

19. The passport was for her work with Médecins du Monde.

20. Alina in San Salvador with Médecins du Monde, 1985

21. Alina and Marek with Leszek Kołakowski
and Tamara Kołakowska, 1970s

22. Working with Médecins du Monde in Chad, 1982; Alina is wearing a Polish Solidarity Movement t-shirt.

23. Alina in the 1980s

24. Alina and Marek in the 1990s

For Product Safety Concerns and Information please contact our
EU representative GPSR@taylorandfrancis.com Taylor & Francis
Verlag GmbH, Kaufingerstraße 24, 80331 München, Germany